The God Who Loves and Is Loved

The God Who Loves and Is Loved

The Vicarious Humanity of Christ and the Response of Love

Christian D. Kettler

CASCADE *Books* • Eugene, Oregon

THE GOD WHO LOVES AND IS LOVED
The Vicarious Humanity of Christ and the Response of Love

Copyright © 2019 Christian D. Kettler. All rights reserved. Except for brief quotations in critical publications or reviews, no part of this book may be reproduced in any manner without prior written permission from the publisher. Write: Permissions, Wipf and Stock Publishers, 199 W. 8th Ave., Suite 3, Eugene, OR 97401.

Cascade Books
An Imprint of Wipf and Stock Publishers
199 W. 8th Ave., Suite 3
Eugene, OR 97401

www.wipfandstock.com

PAPERBACK ISBN: 978-1-4982-8904-7
HARDCOVER ISBN: 978-1-4982-8906-1
EBOOK ISBN: 978-1-4982-8905-4

Cataloguing-in-Publication data:

Names: Kettler, Christian D., 1954–, author.

Title: The God who loves and is loved : the vicarious humanity of Christ and the response of love / Christian D. Kettler.

Description: Eugene, OR : Cascade Books, 2019 | Includes bibliographical references and index.

Identifiers: ISBN 978-1-4982-8904-7 (paperback) | ISBN 978-1-4982-8906-1 (hardcover) | ISBN 978-1-4982-8905-4 (ebook)

Subjects: LCSH: Jesus Christ—Person and offices. | Love—Religious aspects—Christianity.

Classification: BT772 .K48 2019 (print) | BT772 .K48 (ebook)

Manufactured in the U.S.A. NOVEMBER 10, 2019

Scripture quotations are from the New Revised Version of the Bible, copyright © 1989, by the Division of Christian Education of the National Council of the Churches of Christ in the United States of America. Used by permission. All rights reserved.

The following chapters appeared in earlier editions and were granted permission for republication:

Used by permission of Wipf and Stock Publishers: www.wipfandstock.com:

"The Problem with 'Preferential Love': Should Love Depend upon My Initiative? A Challenge for Reformed Theology—An Answer from the Vicarious Humanity of Christ," originally published in *Evangelical Calvinism: Volume 2: Dogmatics and Devotion*, edited by Myk Habets and Bobby Grow (2017).

Used by permission of *Participatio, Journal of the Thomas F. Torrance Theological Fellowship*, www.tftorrance.org:

"Where Are the Fruits of Love? T. F. Torrance, the Vicarious Humanity of Christ, and Ecclesiology," *Participatio: Journal of the Thomas F. Torrance Theological Fellowship*, Vol. 5 (2016) 73–88, accessible at www.tftorrance.org.

To my students in the
Master of Arts in Christian Ministry program
at Friends University
1988–2016

Contents

Acknowledgments xi

Introduction: The Love of the Father for the Son, the Vicarious Love of the Son for the Father in the Spirit 1

1. The Problem with "Preferential Love": Should Love Depend upon My Choosing? 16
2. Can Self-Love Be True Love? 38
3. The "Double Love" of God and Neighbor: How Do Love of God and Love of Neighbor Live Together? 49
4. The Vicarious Love of the Son for Flames, Friends, and Families 69
5. Is Love Essential to Our Humanity? 85
6. Where Are the Fruits of Love? 104

Bibliography 125
Name/Subject Index 131

Acknowledgments

The author would like to gratefully acknowledge the help of the staff of the Edmund Stanley Library of Friends University; bookstore manager Michael Sullivan; the editors of the volume *Evangelical Calvinism*, Myk Habets and Bobby Grow; the editor of *Participatio*, Todd Speidell; the pastor of Bibleway Community of Faith, Jeff Enlow; and the congregration of Bibleway, for their support and contributions to this volume.

Introduction

The Love of the Father for the Son, the Vicarious Love of the Son for the Father in the Spirit

Can there be a greater folly than attempting to write a book about love? C. S. Lewis once wrote a book entitled *The Problem of Pain*, exhibiting excruciating logic to an obviously often ambiguous and emotional issue. His good friend Charles Williams replied that hell was designed for people that write books about the problem of pain! How presumptuous can one be to think that one might write dispassionately about such an issue. Perhaps the same is true about the subject of love. Certainly, who knows enough about it? I readily admit I don't. (Except what I have been taught by my Siamese cats, Linus and Lucy, and a few friends, along with my father and mother.)

If love is a reality, it certainly is an action and just venting words about it can be the ultimate in hypocrisy. Kierkegaard reminds us that love is "sheer action," not words or theory.[1] I am hardly a selfless person. Perhaps that is why I needed to write this book, and why the subject of love is worth thinking and writing about. Maybe that is why you need to read this book. What is the greatest reason for thinking, writing, and reading, than to meditate on the most important subjects? Most of all, as a Christian, and a theologian, at the heart of the faith is the belief that God is love (1 John 4:8).

It has only been a couple of years since I lost both of my parents, Del and Pat Kettler. Many have not been fortunate to have loving parents. However common love of offspring may be in the animal kingdom, that is not necessarily the case with the human being. I am fortunate to be among the

---

1. Kierkegaard, *Works of Love*, 99.

ones who had parents that demonstrated nothing less than unconditional love to me all of my life. There can be no greater motive to write this book than my reflections on that love. Did that love prepare me for the love of God? In his *Confessions*, Augustine famously reflects on his wasteful youth, acknowledging that his single desire "was simply to love and to be loved."[2] How many of us would argue with that fact in our lives? It is tempting to begin a theology methodologically with our human experiences of love, good or bad. Yet if we have learned anything from the theological revolution of Karl Barth, it is that Christian theology should begin with the witness born of the Word of God in the Scriptures, not with human experience, however meaningful it may be.[3] Looking back, I am also more painfully aware of my lack of love toward my parents; in deeds left undone if not done. I know my lack of ability to love. How does the love of God relate to human love, with its experience of richness or lack thereof? Where is Christ, and particularly his obedient life of faith and love toward the Father, in all of this? That is the burden of this book. But be forewarned, we will hardly be able to touch upon every aspect of the idea of love, philosophically or theologically. This will be a limited exercise in Christian dogmatics integrated with ethics: the doctrine of the Son's response to the Father's love, and its implications for our love, what has been called "the vicarious humanity of Christ." That, we will find, will be rich enough.

Do We Do It All for Love?

What motivates the human being? Freud is famous for saying sex. The multidisciplinary thinker Ernest Becker said no, it is the fear of death. All of our activities are "heroic projects" to deny the fact that we are going to die.[4] Even Christian projects of "self-denial," Dietrich Bonhoeffer claims, can easily become "so many single acts of self-martyrdom or ascetic exercises" that are only acts of "the expression of the human person's will."[5] What if both are wrong? What if something is more important to the human being than sex or death? Could that be love, particularly the desire to love and be loved? We have cited Augustine in that regard. Augustine seems very modern in the contemporary equation of love with what we desire. Augustine,

---

2. Augustine, *Confessions*, 3.1.
3. Barth, *CD* I/1 (Second Edition), "Word of God and Experience," 198–227.
4. Becker, *Denial of Death*.
5. Bonhoeffer, *Discipleship*, 86.

Introduction

of course, in his most well-known quote, speaks of the heart that is restless until it finds its rest in God.[6] Yet contemporary desires for money, sex, and power would be far from the great church father's thoughts. Could the desire be for that which we need the most—a genuine kind of love, with its origins in the God revealed in Jesus Christ? This book explores the implications for love of the vicarious humanity of Christ, that Christ represents and takes the place of our humanity. Love may be "all there is, it makes the world go 'round" (Bob Dylan), yet it remains a mystery for us to grasp and even practice.[7] We are tortured by its absence or betrayal, yet we continually go back for more. We seem to know instinctively that to be without love is to be a pauper. Paradoxically, something that can bring so much misery can also bring such great riches.[8] "Jesus Christ *is* our human response to God," T. F. Torrance boldly declares.[9] Therefore, he is also our human response of love, when we are unloved, lacking love, having lost love, or finding it difficult if not impossible to love, as we find ourselves in this often-hostile world.

Karl Barth comments that his fellow theologian Friedrich Schleiermacher so believed in such a close connection between sexual love and religion that, not only did he glorify love and marriage, he also made them the paradigm for religious experience.[10] Do the Catholic and Orthodox churches do any less when they call marriage a sacrament? Is this a high view of marriage, or do both Schleiermacher and Catholicism deny the very human nature of sex, love, and marriage? Is there any religious love that can be purged of all sublimated erotic love? Barth asks.[11] Divine love always comes with the "stuff" of history, sociology, and psychology in human existence. We all bring our personal "histories" to any love.

However, what about the love command of Jesus? Does that not call us to love *all people*? Is that even possible? How do we literally affect the lives of all, especially without doing things that may be motivated by love, but end up with unintended bad consequences? This is surely the truth behind

---

6. Augustine, *Confessions*, 1.1.
7. Dylan, "I Threw It All Away."
8. Kierkegaard, *Works of Love*, 10.
9. T. F. Torrance, *Mediation of Christ*, 80.
10. Barth, *Theology and Church*, 174–75.
11. Barth, *Theology and Church*, 351.

Reinhold Niebuhr's "Christian Realism."[12] In addition, there are so many people, but so little time![13]

Love, Atonement, the Incarnation, and the Vicarious Humanity of Christ

Even a Christ-centered view of love may not be enough. We may easily say, "Jesus loves me," but have a Jesus who is without our humanity. He may surely be God, delivering a divine message or atonement, but, as in the "Christus Victor" theory of atonement, often we see the victory of Christ as only the triumph of the sheer power of deity.[14] We suggest a subtle yet important twist on Christology here. A "double movement," however, is reflected in the incarnation of God in Jesus: from God to humans, and from humans to God, the deity and the humanity of Christ. This is his "vicarious humanity," as Thomas and James Torrance have put it, a humanity lived on our behalf, in our place, vicarious in the totality of Jesus' humanity, not just his death.[15] He is "the hearing man," claims Thomas Torrance, "in a final and definitive way."[16] Knowing God perfectly, he is "the perfect hearer of God" in Karl Barth's words, "the One who knows God perfectly, and therefore, the perfect servant and witness and teacher of God."[17] Even on the cross, he is mocked for his faith: "He trusts in God; let God deliver him now, if he wants to; for he said, 'I am God's Son'" (Matt 27:43). He is final and definitive in terms of faith, worship, and service, but also love. He hears the voice of the Father, the voice of love, and responds with love, on our behalf and in our place. He is our representative and substitute "in all

---

12. See the discussion in Marsden, *Twilight of the American Enlightenment*, 112–25.

13. Ferreira, *Love's Grateful Striving*, 3.

14. See Gregory Boyd in *The Nature of the Atonement: Four Views*, edited by James Beilby and Paul R. Eddy, 23–65, and the classic exposition by Gustav Aulén, *Christus Victor: An Historical Study of the Three Main Types of the Idea of Atonement*.

15. The most important writings on the vicarious humanity of Christ are found in T. F. Torrance, *Mediation of Christ*; T. F. Torrance, "Word of God"; J. B. Torrance, "Vicarious Humanity of Christ"; J. B. Torrance, *Worship, Community and the Triune God of Grace*; Thomas F. Torrance et al., *Passion for Christ*; Torrance, *Incarnation: The Person and Life of Christ*; and T. F. Torrance, *Atonement: The Person and Work of Christ*. Elmer M. Colyer provides a helpful survey of the vicarious humanity of Christ in T. F. Torrance's thought in *How to Read T. F. Torrance*, 97–126.

16. T. F. Torrance, *God and Rationality*, 145.

17. Barth, *CD* IV/2, 409.

our relations with God, including every understanding and knowing, loving and worshipping."[18] This response "thereby invalidates all other ways of response." Torrance is not alone in his thinking here. The young Dietrich Bonhoeffer in his doctoral dissertation, *Sanctorum Communio*, presents the biblical Israelite leader as a "collective person," or *Stellvertretung*, translated "deputyship," or more recently, "vicarious representative action."[19] The vicarious nature of response to God's love has become embedded in the womb of Israel.[20] Therefore, our attempts at love have been invalidated! Is there not a place for our love, then? Only as it is "derived from, grounded in, and shaped by the very humanity of the Word."[21] But can this bold statement stand? How does it do so? As "the collective person," Bonhoeffer reminds us, we stand with sinful Adam as well (Rom 3–6).[22] Christ may represent the people, being a part of who they are, but he also stands in for them, stands in their place in an act of love, doing something they are unable to do.[23]

Love, the Son, and the Father

Christ is "the *beloved* Son" who is baptized and submits to baptism, to the grace of God in his life (Mark 1:9–11; Matt 3:13–17; Luke 3:21–23). In this act of solidarity with sinners, Jesus does not stand distant from humanity, but his love and being loved is on our behalf (representative) and in our place (substitute). His love and being loved is not afraid then of sharing in our fears and doubts, even about love. Does God love us? Do we love God? Do we love anyone truly? Can love be found? And can love last? These are issues that Jesus enters into in his baptism.

Jesus truly lives the life of one who loves God. Love means obedience. This is what distinguished Jesus as the Son of God.[24] He keeps the Father's commandments; he is the one who can keep the exhortations of

---

18. T. F. Torrance, *God and Rationality*, 145.
19. Bonhoeffer, *Sanctorum Communio*, 119–20; See also 145ff and 183ff.
20. The theme of T. F. Torrance, *Mediation of Christ*.
21. T. F. Torrance, *God and Rationality*, 146.
22. Bonhoeffer, *Sanctorum Communio*, 121.
23. Williams, *Bonhoeffer's Black Jesus*, 142n7. Williams may underplay the importance of representation here. Representation is important for Christ to be in solidarity with our humanity.
24. Barth, *CD* IV/1, 164.

the Sermon on the Mount.[25] He lives a life of serving God, not mammon (Matt 6:24; Luke 16:13). In Gethsemane, imploring the Father to remove the cup, he nonetheless accepts that the will of God be done (Matt 26:42; Mark 14:36; Luke 22:42). In a world of many who simply say "Lord, Lord," and do not do the will of the Father (Matt 7:21–23; Luke 6:46; cf. Luke 13:25–27), "here at last is a man who loves the Lord with all his heart and soul and mind and strength and his neighbor as himself."[26] In addition, he is the man who cries out in abandonment on the cross. A cry is made because the Son knows he is beloved and the cross seems to be a contradiction to that. "It is the cry of the child that reveals the mother's heart," John McLeod Campbell reminds us.[27] Nonetheless, the Son loves, and therefore can love for us when we are unable.

This pain of rejection is not only from the Father but also from the world: "He came to what was his own, and his own people did not accept him" (John 1:10). Of course, the precursor for this is God's relationship with Israel. The *crux* of the Old Testament is Yahweh's relationship with Israel: "I will be your God . . . and you shall be my people" is the unilateral decision of covenant made by God. However, Israel seems to frustrate God's purpose, and God seems like the frustrated parent: "When Israel was a child I loved him, and out of Egypt I called my son. The more I called them, the more they went from me" (Hos 11:1–2). As Paul Fiddes comments on these verses: "A loving relationship allows the risk of freedom to the other, and therefore involves pain."[28]

Yet the love of the Son for the Father does not exclude those who follow him from loving like he does. Love and obeying commands are not mutually exclusive. The dependence of the Son on the Father did not rule out exhortations for the disciples to obey his commands. The verses: "A disciple is not above the teacher, nor a slave above the master; it is enough for the disciple to be like the teacher, and the slave like the master" (Matt 10:24–25 and John 13:16; 15:20) exist together with: "Very truly, I tell you," says Jesus, "the Son can do nothing on his own, but what he sees the Father doing; for whatever the Father does, the Son does likewise" (John 5:19). The Son is unable to do anything without the Father, yet because "the Father/Son relation falls within the one being of God" and "there is perfect and

---

25. Thurneysen, *Sermon on the Mount*.
26. Smail, "Can One Man Die for the People?," 87.
27. Campbell, *Nature of the Atonement*, 177.
28. Fiddes, *Participation in God*, 165.

eternal mutuality between the Father and the Son,"[29] the Son is also able to demonstrate the authority of the kingdom of God for the Father, the vicarious *deity* of Christ, if you will: "In claiming that authority and rule as his own, Jesus was in fact putting himself in God's place."[30] As such, he can demand love from his disciples (John 15:12).

Love and the Trinity

The place of Christocentrism opens up for us the triune being of God, the Trinity. A "Supreme Being" is not revealed here, but a fellowship of the Father and the Son, the God who "does not will to be without the Other."[31] "The love which meets us in reconciliation, and then retrospectively in creation, is real love, supreme law and ultimate reality, because God is antecedently love in Himself."[32] This One enables us to participate through the Spirit.[33] Not a being of only "peace and love," Barth says, "but concretely as the Father and the Son, and this is the fellowship, the unity, the peace, the love of the Holy Spirit who is Himself the Spirit of the Father and the Son."[34] What is at stake here? The baptism of Jesus is a disclosure of the immanent, not just economic Trinity, in the baptized Son, the voice of the Father, and the descent of the Spirit like a dove.[35] This reveals, in Karl Barth's words, "God is now not only the electing Creator, but the elect creature. He is not only the giver, but also the recipient of grace. He is not only the One who commands, but the One who is called and pledged to obedience."[36] Jesus is the recipient of grace! This obedience, this oneness of mind between the Father and the Son, reveals Jesus as the Son of God.[37] Thomas Smail strikes a cosmological spark: When in Gethsemane, we look in "the mirror of his (Jesus') suffering humanity we are looking right into the central secret of

---

29. T. F. Torrance, *Trinitarian Faith*, 119.
30. T. F. Torrance, *Christian Doctrine of God*, 46.
31. Barth, *CD* I/1(Second Edition), 483.
32. Barth, *CD* I/1 (Second Edition), 483–84.
33. Barth, *CD* I/1 (Second Edition), 483.
34. Barth, *CD* IV/2, 341.
35. Hart, *Beauty of the Infinite*, 168
36. Barth, *CD* IV/1, 170.
37. Barth, *CD* IV/1, 164.

the universe, into the heart of God where the Father and Son express in endless richness their mutual self-giving, the one to the other."[38]

The central secret of the universe! What is that secret but the mutual love between the Father and the Son in the Spirit that exists eternally, now being made manifest in the life of Jesus of Nazareth? That mutuality, a "double movement of grace," if you will, of love between the Father and the Son through the Spirit in the Trinity has been demonstrated in the incarnation. "God so loved the world" (John 3:16). So love begins with grace, a movement of love, not conditioned by whether or not the beloved responds rightly. Nonetheless, this is very dangerous for human beings to do, for we cannot count on reciprocity. (There would not be any blues or country music if that were so!) Only God can do this, and he does this for us, in the vicarious response of Christ, despite the "unrequited love" he has given humanity as represented by his chosen people, Israel, as Ezekiel reminds us: "Mortal, I am sending you to the people of Israel, to a nation of rebels who have rebelled against me" (Ezek 2:3). This is ultimately true of God's incarnation himself in Jesus: "He was in the world, and the world came into being through him; yet the world did not know him. He came to what was his own, and his own people did not accept him" (John 1:10–11).

Love, the Trinity, and the Nature of God

Our common practice of loving is that we try to make love secure by having expectations or conditions, a "no-risk" love. No, God is free to risk, for love means vulnerability. For the beloved always has the potential to devastate the lover, by loss or retreat from the lover. "Our deepest feelings," Ray Anderson reminds us, "are often invested in that which has the capacity to break our hearts."[39] The nature of *eros* is essentially "tragic" and "melancholy," Barth claims, because of the "alternation of possession and loss, intoxication and soberness, enthusiasm and disillusionment."[40] Dare we spare God of such a love, especially the triune God, despite Barth's refusal? The gratuitousness of God's love in Christ is distinct from a "works righteousness" of love, by which we give our love as a condition in order to coerce someone to love us. The very nature of the Holy Spirit as God is God the Giver coming as sent by the Father through the Son as Gift. The

---

38. Smail, *Forgotten Father*, 104.
39. Anderson, *Unspoken Wisdom*, 53.
40. Barth, *CD* IV/2, 788.

Introduction

Holy Spirit is no abstract gift, but God in person.[41] However, the Father does not coerce Jesus to respond with love. He does this for us, as a vicarious act. This was a free act on his part. (Barth unfortunately rejects *eros* as opposed to this freedom.) The Son has taken on the risk of loving God the Father for us. As Barth will say, God's freedom and love act together.[42] So, by appropriation, God's "freedom" may be seen as the first movement of the "double movement" of the incarnation, the "humanward" movement to become human, a freedom to become human, for the sake of the second movement, the "Godward" movement of the Son's love toward the Father in the vicarious humanity, or response of Christ.[43]

Do we have the basis for what is truly divine love in human form in this "economic" manifestation of the Trinity, and therefore the ground and possibility for *our* acts of love? He is also the "immanent" or "ontological" Trinity, the One who loves eternally as Father, Son, and Spirit, "the original source of every I and Thou."[44] There is actual knowledge of God as triune love that has been revealed in the incarnation. In Barth's words, God as Trinity is "revealer, revelation, and revealedness."[45] And this being is known in the act of the incarnation: "If we really want to understand revelation in terms of its subject, i.e., God, then the first thing we have to realize is that this subject, God, the Revealer, is identical with His act in revelation and also identical with its effect."[46] This is genuine knowledge of God, but that does not mean it is exhaustive knowledge of God.[47] It is knowledge that comes from the covenant of grace, therefore it is inaccessible by us on our own efforts, but a wonderful reality by the act of God in Christ.[48] John McLeod Campbell puts it in a most moving way: "Let us see the Fatherly heart as yet unrevealed—waiting to be revealed. Let us contemplate the Son as coming forth to reveal it."[49] This is "God antecedent in the atonement."

---

41. Barth, *CD* I/1 (Second Edition), 489.

42. Barth, *CD* I/2, 257–350.

43. For a critical doctrine of appropriations in regards to the Trinity that nonetheless maintains mutuality (*perichoresis*), see Torrance, *Christian Doctrine of God*, 200 and Barth, *CD* I/1 (Second Edition), 353ff.

44. Barth, *CD* III/2, 218.

45. Barth, *CD* I/1 (Second Edition) 295.

46. Barth, *CD* I/1 (Second Edition), 296.

47. See the discussion in Molnar, *Divine Freedom*.

48. Barth, *CD* IV/1, 45. Cf. 45: "Grace is inaccessible to us; how else can it be grace? Grace can only make itself accessible."

49. Campbell, *Nature of the Atonement*, 177.

In addition, when God becomes incarnate, can he avoid the tragedies that are essential to living in human community? As Ray Anderson ponders: "There is something inherently tragic about the form of our present community of human love. We have presence to each other only through the present reality of discontinuity. No other person is ever totally 'at hand' to us."[50] Will this be helpful as we continue to face the perennial challenges of human love? Will it be helpful in understanding the relationship between divine love and romantic and friendship love? Will we be able to have a constructive relationship between divine love and sexual love, with all of the challenges that contemporary desires bring to that most emotional and perplexing of issues? Will it help us to understand (and practice) the Lord's injunction to "love your enemies"? Will we be able to see a surer foundation for justice coming out of the Son's love for the Father, rather than justice as simply jockeying for a position against love, as in most traditional ethics? The list goes on.

The Freedom of God as Humanward

Even with understanding the freedom of God as being "more proper" to the Father (the humanward movement) than the Son is, nonetheless the mutuality, or *perichoresis,* between the Father, the Son, and the Holy Spirit should remind us that we should also speak of the humanward movement as the love of the Father as well. Again, "for God so loved world that he gave his one and only Son" (John 3:16). Nevertheless, the truth of the unity of God should not neglect the differentiation in God, such as the Son's eternal response to the Father of love. What does this mean, then, for how human beings experience the love of God, particularly through the incarnation of the Son in Jesus Christ? Something particular has happened in the "economic" revelation of God in the incarnation, but it should reflect at least some of what is going on from all eternity between the three persons of the "immanent" Trinity. Again, the economic Trinity is a genuine, yet not exhaustive, revelation of the immanent Trinity, who God is in himself.

The sovereignty of God should not be contemplated apart from Jesus Christ. This sovereignty is sovereign love because it is trinitarian. We understand the incarnation as the initiative of God's sovereign love, not as a need in the triune God, either to love or to create. Nor is love anything

---

50. Anderson, *On Being Human,* 177.

human beings can demand. "Love is an ultimate fact and knows no 'Why.'"⁵¹ What we do know is that reconciliation comes out of the prior love of God, as Calvin teaches.⁵²

Since creation is an action that God did not need to make, we view the *ex nihilo* in the amazing fact that God expresses his freedom in his ability to become the creature in the incarnation. How much more will that be true in his ability to vicariously take on the tortured humanity of his creature and replace it with his holiness in the vicarious humanity of Christ, the "double movement of grace" (how Calvin beautifully speaks of justification and sanctification, but this can be seen to be much broader and deeper ontologically in our humanity)?⁵³

Christ's Love as Godward

We have demonstrated the contrast between our inabilities to love with God's perfect love. In the incarnation, God himself comes to fulfill the law, in Christ. "Christ is of the end of the law" (Rom 10:4). Surely Paul means either "goal" or "fulfillment" in the sense of Matthew 5:17: "Do not think that I have come to abolish the law or the prophets; I have come not to abolish but to fulfill."⁵⁴ A meaning of Christ as the termination of the law seems unlikely, although Kierkegaard can speak of the "downfall" of the law because of Christ.⁵⁵ Christ is the one who satisfied the "thirst," so the law only exists now as "perfect fulfillment." As either "goal" or "fulfillment," Christ does what we have been unable to do: keep the law of God. Does this mean, however, that keeping of the law was a requirement for Christ to receive the love of the Father? Certainly aspects of some Reformed "covenant theology" seems to imply so.⁵⁶ Yet, as Kierkegaard argues, Christ fulfilling the law only demonstrates that he does what the law was unable to do, "Whereas the law with its requirement became everyone's downfall because they were not what it required and through it only learned to know sin. Christ then

---

51. Torrance, *Doctrine of Jesus Christ*, 87.
52. Calvin, *Institutes*, 2.16.4.
53. Barth, *CD* IV/1, 317; Calvin, *Institutes*, 3.11.1.
54. But see the long discussion on differing views of Romans 10:4 in Cranfield, *Romans*, 515–20.
55. Kierkegaard, *Works of Love*, 99.
56. See Allen, *Christ's Faith*, 163–65.

became the downfall of the Law; because he was what it required."[57] The radical righteousness of Christ is something he does now "apart from law" (Rom 3:21), an extremely important verse in Romans. The "requirement" Christ submitted to was not to win the Father's love, but to take our place. Thus, there is "an eternal difference" between Christ and the Christian.[58]

However, this "eternal difference" is that which enables Christ to be with us. He is the only one who loves God purely, and he does so for us and in our place. "In love to God man is not alone," Barth comments. "On the contrary, in love to God he has to do with a genuine partner—with the One who loving Him first has given Himself to be his own, and therefore made Himself a genuine partner."[59]

Such "Godward" action is the heart of the vicarious humanity of Christ, the second movement of the incarnation. In this, Jesus Christ demonstrates the harmony of freedom and obedience that is the truth of God making us in his image, not Adam's disharmony.[60] The true basis of the Lord's command to serve, Barth contends, is not just in the command but also in his own fulfillment of it in Jesus Christ.[61] He has taken the form of the slave (Phil 2:7) (at least economically; herein is the disagreement between Barth on one side and Torrance and Molnar on the other. Barth holds to an eternal obedience of the Son; Torrance sees in that the dangers of subordinationism).[62]

Bonhoeffer's concept of *Stellvertretung* ("vicarious representative action") does not so much declare solidarity as bring judgment upon Israel when Christ fulfills the law by love, overcoming the Jewish understanding of the law.[63] No longer does God simply exclude the willful transgressor of Israel, but now all of Israel has fallen away from God, along with the humanity of Adam. It now must be resurrected in a new community united under the person of Christ. The church itself is, sociologically as well as theologically, a unique community because of the principle of vicarious

---

57. Kierkegaard, *Works of Love*, 99.
58. Kierkegaard, *Works of Love*, 101.
59. Barth, *CD* I/2, 388.
60. Smail, *Like Father, Like Son*, 175.
61. Barth, *CD* III/4, 662.
62. See the discussion in Kettler, *Vicarious Humanity of Christ*, 95–97, on the side of Barth. See also Molnar (siding with T. F. Torrance) against Barth in "Obedience of the Son in the Theology of Karl Barth," 313–54.
63. Bonhoeffer, *Sanctorum Communio*, 148.

representative action. Its ethic of neighborliness transcends other boundaries of in- or outgroups, conscience, or responsibility.[64] Joachim von Soosten sees this action of one on behalf of the many, of vicarious representative action, to be the center of Bonhoeffer's justification of his conspiratorial activities against the Nazis, as seen in his contemporaneous thoughts in his *Ethics* and the *Letters and Papers from Prison*. In prison, this is interpreted in terms of a radical theology of the cross, a theological criticism of religion which undermines the metaphysical concept of God, and a "nonreligious" view of the world, all understood in light of vicarious representative action.[65]

Our Loves

Furthermore, Kierkegaard identifies erotic and friendship love as only self-love, different from divine love. Love is not based on the object and the demands of the object unless it has the right to be God.[66] The object of erotic or friendship love cannot be "everything" to the lover. Christ is "the explainer" who is "the explanation," for whom we can only gain humility, the humility that reduces us to "nothing."[67] This is not a "worm theology," humans are worth less than worms, but an expression of our very creation, which came from nothing, an act of God's grace. Living in this humility is the opposite of the one who "forgets" God.[68] You may be well off and manage to become something, yet you may forget your very creation and the One to whom you owe everything. Thus, it is easy to become "noisy along with the crowd" and "be busy from morning until night," busily forgetting God. Yet, by not holding fast to God, one ironically loses "everything," "inasmuch the world cannot take everything, simply because it cannot give everything." "Every person is God's bond servant; therefore he dare not belong to anyone in love unless in the same love he belongs to God . . . —a person dare not belong to another as if that other person were everything to him; a person dare not allow another to belong to him as if he were everything to that other."[69] In our proposal, only Christ in his vicarious humanity

---

64. von Soosten, "Editor's Afterword," 304–5.
65. von Soosten, "Editor's Afterword," 305.
66. Kierkegaard, *Works of Love*, 107–8.
67. Kierkegaard, *Works of Love*, 101.
68. Kierkegaard, *Works of Love*, 102.
69. Kierkegaard, *Works of Love*, 107–8.

has a love for others that first belongs to a love of the Father. Can our erotic and friendship love be "the same love" in which one "belongs to God"?

The Grace of God and Our Loves

What Kierkegaard is speaking of here is, of course, the grace of God. The only One who can "give everything" is God, "who takes everything, everything, everything—in order to give everything—who does not piecemeal take little or much or exceedingly much but takes infinitely everything if you truly hold fast to him."[70] For Barth, Paul puts it plainly in Philippians 1:21: "For to me, living is Christ and dying is gain." Our lives have become "arrested and confiscated" by Christ's life.[71] So Paul can speak of his life and ministry as "always carrying in the body the death of Jesus, so that the life of Jesus may also be made visible in our bodies" (2 Cor 4:10). This is the new creation in Christ (2 Cor 5:17), or the hidden life with Christ in God (Col 3:3), where Christians live by the faith of the Son of God who loved me and gave himself up for me (Gal 2:20). "Christ lives vicariously for me, as it could be summed up."[72]

This does not mean either a radical separation between *agape* (gift-love) and *eros* (need-love), or a blurring of the distinction between the two. Certainly, the vicarious humanity of Christ speaks of the grace of God coming into our lives to conform our desires to his, our loves and longings to his, as James K. A. Smith has recently written, echoing Augustine.[73] However, the issue is not simply in reorienting your loves: once you loved possessions, now you love God. No, our situation is much graver. We need to be uprooted at the level of ontology, at the level of our being, by the vicarious humanity of Christ.

Divine love, however, does not seek to control or be coercive, but, ironically, controls oneself.[74] In contrast is the "toxic love" of pure desire, seeking to create love in the other person, but in doing so, denying the other's freedom.[75] True freedom is based on God's own freedom. Similarly, Karl Barth argues against a "middle knowledge" view of the providence of

---

70. Kierkegaard, *Works of Love*, 103.
71. Barth, *Epistle to the Philippians*, 37.
72. Barth, *Epistle to the Philippians*, 37.
73. Smith, *You Are What You Love*, 2.
74. Kierkegaard, *Works of Love*, 217.
75. Kierkegaard, *Works of Love*, 221–22.

Introduction

God that denies God's freedom, by stressing the all-encompassing reality of grace, even in the midst of our free will. Nothing is between grace and our free will. Even the hypothetical thoughts of what we might do in a certain circumstance with our free will are irrelevant. The "middle knowledge" view of Molina in the seventeenth century and William Craig and others in our day still insists that God's will is an accomplished "middle knowledge." Still God is "limited" by a certain number of choices in this view.[76] It is folly to try to lay down "conditions" on God, especially to be conditioned by our so-called free will. We understand our free will (and, indeed, our humanity) in the context of grace as a person, the person of Jesus Christ, the One for whom obedience and freedom, grace and free will, were not antithetical to each other. Now, let T. F. Torrance and Karl Barth send us forth with these most fitting words: "All of grace means all of man."[77] "Where grace is not extolled, there can only be sin. There is no third possibility."[78]

---

76. Barth, *CD* II/1, 585.

77. Torrance, *Mediation of Christ*, xii.

78. Barth, *CD* II/1, 586.

CHAPTER ONE

The Problem with "Preferential Love"

Should Love Depend upon My Choosing?

"You did not choose me, but I chose you." (John 15:16)

Reformed theology is distinctive in its love for the doctrine of election. Election means that salvation begins with the grace of God. However, how does election not become deterministic or coercive when it comes to love? If love does not coerce, it is free. What Kierkegaard calls "preferential love" is the love of choice. We choose to love another, choose to desire them, to "possess" them. Kierkegaard sees this as inferior to divine love. Is this true when we consider the love of the Son for the Father on our behalf (the vicarious *love* of Christ, we may call it)?

Surely, the Son chooses to be faithful and obedient, to love the Father. " My food is to do the will of him who sent me and to complete his work," Jesus says in the Gospel of John (4:34; cf. 6:38; 7:18; 8:50; 9:4; 10:37; 12:49–50; 14:31; 15:10—"just as I have kept my Father's commandments and abide in his love;" 17:4). The Son does only that which he sees the Father doing, because the Father loves the Son (5:19–20). He knows that he is "my Son, the beloved" (Matt 3:1: Mark 1:11; Luke 3:22).

This freedom, however, is unique, a "royal" freedom in Barth's words, consisting of a "conformity with God Himself" as "the secret of the

The Problem with "Preferential Love"

character of Jesus."[1] This "royalty" is seen in that among other human beings he is "*the* man for them."[2] "And this in spite of their own Adamic form; and therefore in spite of their own estrangement and fundamental error in respect of what they think to be good and true and beautiful and comforting and helpful and liberating and redemptive."[3]

The choice of love involves a risk, which is accentuated by the sufferings of Christ, and ultimately the cross. The risks of love involve a choice. What will be Jesus' fate if he loves the Father? Will the Father return the Son's love? What will that love mean? Therefore, these very human questions of the risk of love become the questions of the Son. Will he be able to be our "pioneer and perfecter" of love as well as of faith (Heb 12:2), daring the risk of love that we are unable to risk?

Therefore, his first public appearance, as Barth points out, is as a penitent, confessing sins (even though he did not have any) by submitting himself to the baptism of John "in unreserved solidarity with other penitents" (Matt 3:13–17; Mark 1:9–11; Luke 3:21–22).[4] As the Heidelberg Catechism, Question 37 states, Jesus "throughout his life on earth . . . (bore) the wrath of God against the sin of the whole human race."[5]

The Distinct Will of the Son

Involved in this is a genuine, distinct will of the Son. Our very participation in the life of God, Paul Fiddes contends, is based on "leaning" on his willing response to the Father, "his 'Yes, Amen,' to the Father's purpose."[6] This becomes a critical action for the church in combatting conformity to the culture. Despite challenges in the history of theology (Monothelitism), the distinct human will of Jesus is clearly seen in Gethsemane, in "one who in every respect has been tested as we are" (Heb 4:15), who "learned obedience through what he suffered" (Heb 5:8).

Yet this is not to deny the union between the Father and the Son. T. F. Torrance, thinking about Athanasius, sees the union of the Son with the

---

1. Barth, *CD* IV/2, 172.
2. Barth, *CD* IV/2, 180.
3. Barth, *CD* IV/2, 180.
4. Barth, *CD* IV/1, 165.
5. *The Heidelberg Catechism* from Cochrane, ed., *Reformed Confessions of the Sixteenth Century*, 311.
6. Fiddes, *Participation in God*, 53.

Father as essential for a genuine knowledge of God, "The really decisive point for Athanasius is that in Jesus Christ it is God himself who has come among us savingly to make our existence and hurt his own, without ceasing to be what he is in his eternal reality."[7] "God so *loved* the world..." (John 3:16) means that God the Father loves with all that implies. Jayber Crow, Wendell Berry's barber in the novel of the same name, speaks of this love as "compassion, the taking offense, the disappointment, the anger, the bearing of wounds, the weeping of tears."[8] The impassibility and immutability of God must not be understood as God unable to move himself or incapable of passion. God's serenity and tranquility in the face of any situation is "nevertheless the living, self-moving God who is in his own fullness a communion of love."[9] This is a free love and creates freedom for human beings. God the Father acts freely yet not coercively, even upon the Son. Human beings cannot make themselves free, only God does this when humans are born of God's Word and Spirit as God's covenant-partners.[10] Therefore, there is nothing that the human can do to condition or limit God. The free love, yet obedience, of the Son reminds us of this.

In other words, the will of the Son as expressed in the vicarious humanity of Christ is not in competition with his deity but an expression of that eternal "communion of love" that reaches down to humanity, making the response of love we are unable to make. The Son "chooses," yes, but only as a manifestation of, in Torrance's phrase, the "being" of God that can only be known in his "act."[11] Love has ontological roots, as the act of God known in his being. Apart from this, would be the implication "that God is not in himself what he is toward us through the Son and in the Spirit."[12] The Son's "choice" may offer an answer to Kierkegaard's critique that preferential love is not divine love but only self-love. He seems right, however, to identify many problems in the practice of love as simply our choice.

---

7. T. F. Torrance, *Divine and Contingent Order*, 7.
8. Berry, *Jayber Crow*, 251.
9. T. F. Torrance, *Divine and Contingent Order*, 6.
10. Barth, *CD* IV/3.1, 447.
11. T. F. Torrance, *Divine and Contingent Order*, 7.
12. T. F. Torrance, *Divine and Contingent Order*, 7.

The Problem with "Preferential Love"

Love and Hate as Friends?

One may think they are choosing love, but ending up with its opposite, hate. I have written previous books on faith and joy, coupling them with their "problem": doubt for faith and despair for joy. In this book on love, I was tempted to find an "opposite" or "problem" for love. I cannot do that. The opposite of love is not hate. Hate does not deserve to be an opposite to love, because God's triune nature as Father, Son, and Holy Spirit so supremely lives in an eternal quality of its own as a relationship of love.

However, what about hate? Hate, nonetheless, is very close, too close, to love, in human experience. Kierkegaard observes that preferential or "spontaneous" love can be quickly changed into hate, as reflected in the biblical reprimand of James on the misuse of the tongue: "With it we bless the Lord and Father, and with it we curse those who are made in the likeness of God" (James 3:9). Why is this so? Ray Anderson suggests that we are incorrect to see instances of abuse in families as reflections of a lack of love.[13] The fact that most female murder victims will be murdered by a husband or boyfriend is sobering and revealing.[14] How can hateful abuse be borne by a genuine love? Just as we are never betrayed except by someone we love, existentially and emotionally love and hate exist on the same line of continuum.[15]

Choosing to Love: An Act of Justice or Love Expressed as Justice?

The relationship between love and justice becomes crucial here. Are they in tension with one another, as is traditionally thought in ethical theory, or is there some other more harmonious relationship? Nicholas Wolterstorff is an untiring advocate of the harmony between love and justice.[16] For him, there is no tension between love and justice. In fact, relationships between love and justice are "malformations of love" that are represented by injustice such as in unjust generosity and unjust paternalism.[17] But is love only another way of saying justice for Wolterstorff? Is there not an eternal relation of love in the triune God in a way that creates justice? Wolterstorff is

---

13. Anderson, *Self-Care*, 121ff.
14. Anderson, *Self-Care*, 122.
15. For a discussion of betrayal and love, see Anderson, *Self-Care*, 166–83.
16. See Wolterstorff, *Justice in Love*, viii.
17. Wolterstorff, *Justice in Love*, ix.

surely correct that love and justice should not be seen as merely two eternal ideas in tension. However, does he have a preconceived definition of justice in which love finds its definition?

"Agapism," as led by the famous work of Anders Nygren, *Agape and Eros*, has viewed *agape* as "the totality of one's orientation toward one's fellow human being."[18] (Wolterstorff adds that Barth objects to what he sees as determinism here.) In contrast, in a curious way Wolterstorff argues that "love incorporates justice," giving the impression that love and justice still exist as separate spheres that just have to be joined together.[19] One has already defined what "justice" is, apart from love. Love seeks "to promote the good in someone's life as an end in itself," which would include treating one justly and respecting one's rights.[20] This is all well and good, but does one always know what the good is for another? Assuming one does is always the mistake Wolterstorff has previously called "unjust paternalism," of which the greatest practitioner may be the state. (Think of a Veterans Affairs office that routinely ignores desperately ill veterans, so that it would have a good record for fellow bureaucrats.) In fact, Wolterstorff can say that "to treat her as one does because justice requires us to love her."[21] Therefore, love becomes simply distribution of a pre-conceived concept of justice carried out with the optimism that one knows what is best for another. As a caveat, the vicarious humanity of Christ suggests that Christ taking on the entirety of our humanity for us to participate in the entirely of his humanity is a judgment on our preconceived ideas of being human (see also chapter five). Yes, Wolterstorff continues, this includes a judgment on one's worth, yet that only repeats the objection to be aired: On what basis do we say that human beings have worth? Wolterstorff can include an "armistice" between *agape* and *eros* at this point, arguing that "love thus incorporates *eros*," and is worth giving because *eros* is "attraction-love." Yet surely my preference for chocolate over vanilla ice cream does not convey any ontological worth to chocolate ice cream, let alone over vanilla ice cream. It is merely an instance of taste. This seems far from the love of Christ for those who were even his "enemies" (Rom 5:10). Wolterstorff seems to speak of a kind of pragmatic or utilitarian love, loving someone because of their utility, similar to the worship based on ulterior motives that James Torrance contrasts

18. Wolterstorff, *Justice in Love*, ix.
19. Wolterstorff, *Justice in Love*, 93.
20. Wolterstorff, *Justice in Love*, 93.
21. Wolterstorff, *Justice in Love*, 93.

with worship that is based on participation in the Son's communion with the Father.[22] Of course, much of this goes back to Augustine's discussion of the tension between utilitarian *(uti)* and enjoyable *(frui)* love.[23]

Love as an emotion—when it perceives an injustice done to it—can easily become hate. In a tragic sense, love, instead of being the source of justice, is trumped by a demand for the wronging of the individual's "rights" to be rectified. A "moral paradox" occurs in "the sense of moral outrage felt when denied what is perceived as necessary to self-identity (self-esteem) and the abusive (immoral) behavior that results."[24] When one can "choose" love, one can just as easily "choose" to hate. (The maniacal "preacher" played by Robert Mitchum in the film, *The Night of the Hunter*, comes to mind. On one hand is inscribed on his knuckles "love," but on the other is "hate."[25] His behavior vacillates between the two.) The response to such abusive behavior, Anderson contends, should not be simply disapproval or punishment, but a restoration of the self-image. The possibility of forgiveness implies a judgment.[26] A wrong has been done, even against a loved one. The victim needs an "advocate" that will righteously pronounce the verdict, which Christ the Judge, God incarnate has done.[27] Also, at this point, we cannot but think of the purpose of the incarnation, not only as an act of God in humanity, but also as the vicarious response of Christ, as the "recapitulation" or "retelling" of the broken story of Adam by the New Adam, the Son, Jesus Christ (Irenaeus, the great church father of the second century).[28] Essential for the restoration of the self-image is to find ourselves "in Christ," the great Pauline motif.[29] This is an empowerment of the self that must come from outside the self, but nonetheless identifies with our humanity; he is "the Word made flesh" (John 1:14).[30]

---

22. J. B. Torrance, *Worship, Community, and the Triune God of Grace*, 70–71.

23. Augustine, *On Christian Teaching*, 16–17.

24. Anderson, *Self-Care*, 128.

25. *The Night of the Hunter*. United Artists. Directed by Charles Laughton, 1955.

26. Anderson, *Self-Care*, 134ff.

27. Anderson, *Self-Care*, 137.

28. Irenaeus, *Against Heresies*, 5.1.2, 527: "For He (Christ) would not have been one truly possessing flesh and blood, by which He redeemed us, unless He had summed up in Himself the ancient formation of Adam."

29. Stewart, *A Man in Christ: The Vital Elements of St. Paul's Religion*.

30. Anderson, *Self-Care*, 138.

The Imperative of Preferential Love

There are both problems and limitations for "preferential" love, yet it cannot be avoided. Did not the Son "choose" to love the Father, if we take distinctions between the three persons of the Trinity seriously? Is the key to be found in the doctrine of *election*, that the Son loves because he is first loved by the Father? Jesus Christ is the Elect One of God (Barth).[31] He loves because he was loved first. So it is with us (1 John 4:19). The love of the Son trusts in the love of the Father, despite the cross. The love of God in the cross is not overwhelming, as in epiphanies, mystical revelations, and miracles. These manifestations always have a tendency to "coerce" love; a love you cannot deny. Yet coercive love ends up as no love at all, as all overzealous lovers discover. The cross as suffering is the love of the broken heart.[32] The love of the Son for the Father is the "preference" or choice of love that loves because he is loved by the Father. In contrast to our loves, there is no possibility of disillusionment, in spite of the cross.[33] If there is a cry of abandonment from the cross, it is because the Son knows he is loved by the Father and in his humanity cannot reconcile that love to the cross; but he knows that he is loved. Forsakenness, rejection, and betrayal are only realities if there has already been love. We can only be betrayed by those whom we love.[34] The Son's choice is to lament, "My God, my God, why have you forsaken me?" because he is not afraid to take our questions unto himself. This is clearly the connection between mercy and love. Mercy is the love that makes a choice to be merciful, yet is not unjust generosity nor unjust paternalism. In fact, Kierkegaard can speak of mercifulness as being "able to do nothing," for charitable giving includes how it is given (as Clement of Alexandria points out in "The Rich Man's Salvation": one can give away all of one's possessions and still not get rid of "the passions of the soul"[35]). So also, according to Kierkegaard, the one who loves on the behalf of the dead (!) does so without any influence. The dead one can do nothing to reward the one who loves. This is a truly unselfish love.[36] Can this be a challenge to much Christian "busyness" or "activism"?

31. Barth, *CD* II/2, 94, 116–20.
32. Berry, *Jayber Crow*, 254.
33. Barth, *CD* IV/2, 789.
34. Anderson, *Self-Care*, 168.
35. Kierkegaard, *Works of Love*, 323. Clement of Alexandria, "The Rich Man's Salvation," 452
36. Kierkegaard, *Works of Love*, 349.

The Problem with "Preferential Love"

Thomas Torrance makes it plain what a robust Christology must say: "He came in order to embody in himself both our questions to God and God's answers to us, as well as God's questions to us and true answers from us to God."[37] The Son's laments are vicarious. He laments, he complains, if you will, so that we can lament, we can complain. Lament and complaint are only valid if one is loved. This is a robust form of Christ being "in our place," the substitutionary atonement, not just "in our place," as the punishment for our sins in a solely penal form of substitution.[38]

This was the love, not of the one who says, "If you will not love me, then I will hate you," but of the One who says, "If you hate me, I will still continue to love you." Does not preferential love come into its own at this point, *pace* Kierkegaard? God chooses or "elects" to love sinful humanity through the election of his Son, Jesus Christ. Love has a freedom to love, even in a divine sense. The Son's "preference" for the Father makes sense because he has already been the object of the Father's love. What does this mean for humanity? Christ loves in our place because we need to be able to love despite our ungratefulness and the ambiguities of living in a world that is both beautiful and terrible. We need his love to stand in our place, as well as to represent us before the Father, a vicarious love. This is the kind of love that can "recapitulate" (Irenaeus) our frail attempts at preferential love while enabling us to participate in his love. This is especially significant when we do not have or even lose another's preferential love! As we have noted, that can happen even when the deep love changes to equally deep hate.

According to Kierkegaard, preferential love begins with freedom but ends up dependent.[39] Like his synthesis of human existence into both freedom and necessity, the preferential lover finds oneself in despair.[40] What begins as an act of choice, of glorious freedom, ends in a dependency, that one "cannot live without the other." This contrasts with love as a duty, for in that command, "You shall love your neighbor as yourself," there is found true freedom, even though it comes through a command.

---

37. T. F. Torrance, *Theology in Reconstruction*, 122.

38. This is in contrast to Oliver Crisp's "penal" form of the vicarious humanity of Christ, in which the penal aspect becomes the sole nature of the vicarious humanity, thus, in effect, reverting back to a "vicarious death" view. See "John McLeod Campbell and Non-penal Substitution," 92–115. See also J. I. Packer, "What Did the Cross Achieve? The Logic of Penal Substitution," 3–45.

39. Kierkegaard, *Works of Love*, 37–38.

40. Kierkegaard, *Sickness unto Death*, 13–14.

From our perspective, however, this freedom yet in the context of obedience (command) is supremely seen in the humanity of Jesus Christ, the only One who is both free and obedient. In this humanity is the clue to what it truly means to be human, and therefore, what it truly means to love and to be loved.

Preferential Love as Passion

Does the passion of preferential love (erotic love and friendship) account for its genuineness? asks Kierkegaard.[41] Long before Freud, Kierkegaard admits that this kind of love is based on "inclinations" or even "drives." Nonetheless, Christianity is no more scandalized by the sex drive than it is by the need for food and drink.[42] Originally, the poets spoke of erotic love in terms of the passion of loving the one and only beloved, an exclusive love. Christianity certainly challenges that when it commands "love your neighbor"; that means an unconditional love for the ones we meet, a very particular love. Ironically, like the lackadaisical love of "Christendom," the poets now have forsaken the tension of passion. They now grant that erotic love is not exclusive, but one can love many times, and have many different beloveds. In the same way, Christian love as not excluding anyone potentially in "Christendom" includes "when a great many are loved," a kind of promiscuous love.[43] The similarity between his despised "Christendom" and a whorehouse must not be far for Kierkegaard!

Passion is seen to be indispensable to love. That is why the poet views the Christian command to love as "fatuousness" and "preposterous talk," dethroning the place of "inclinations."

However, should Kierkegaard so quickly discount the place of passion in love? Certainly, by relation, one must see the root of "passion" in "compassion." Ray Anderson rightly critiques the long-held interpretation of *agape* as "disinterested love."[44] One thing can be said for the God of the Bible is that he is not "disinterested"! Yet he is not capricious like the gods of the ancient Near East or of Greek and Roman mythology. Being passionate for him is different from being promiscuous. "The love of God is passionate but not promiscuous," Anderson writes. "God loves intensely but not

---

41. Kierkegaard, *Works of Love*, 49ff.
42. Kierkegaard, *Works of Love*, 52.
43. Kierkegaard, *Works of Love*, 50.
44. Anderson, *The Soul of God*, 78.

The Problem with "Preferential Love"

indiscriminately."[45] This is obvious in the book of Hosea, where God cries, "How can I give you up, Ephraim? How can I hand you over, O Israel? . . . My heart recoils within me; my compassion grows warm and tender" (Hos 11:8). Animals mate indiscriminately, but human beings, made in the image of God, do not just mate, but meet.[46] Passion is essential in the encounter between human males and females because of this meeting. No "disinterestedness" here! Mating is simply reflected in promiscuity, animal or human. This is why promiscuity for human beings is ultimately so dehumanizing. Yet to be "religious" is not to surrender passion! Kierkegaard recognizes this himself in his re-telling of the sacrifice of Isaac, *Fear and Trembling*: "The essentially human is passion . . . But the highest passion in a person is faith."[47] Kierkegaard, of course, is thinking of Abraham's passion in being faithful to God, despite the "teleological suspension of the ethical" in intending to heed God's command to sacrifice Isaac.[48] "Love indeed has its priests in the poets, and occasionally we hear a voice that knows how to honor it, but not a word is heard about faith."[49] Kierkegaard, however, does not call on Christianity to despise *eros* or friendship, but to admit that, being preferential loves, they are only forms of self-love.[50] Our interest, as well, is in the vicarious *love* of Christ as integrally related to his vicarious *faith*.

The Vicarious Love of Christ

In response, we may say that the Son's love for the Father is exclusive for the sake of being inclusive, "the One for the Many" (James Torrance).[51] The uniqueness of Christ is One who is for the Many, for through his incarnation we come to share in his personal union with the Father.[52] His devotion

---

45. Anderson, *The Soul of God*, 78.
46. Anderson, *On Being Human*, 53.
47. Kierkegaard, *Fear and Trembling*, 121.
48. Kierkegaard, *Fear and Trembling*, 54–67.
49. Kierkegaard, *Fear and Trembling*, 32.
50. Kierkegaard, *Words of Love*, 52–53.
51. J. B. Torrance, "The Vicarious Humanity of Christ," 137–41 and *Worship, Community and the Triune God of Grace*, 50–67.
52. J. B. Torrance, *Worship, Community and the Triune God of Grace*, 51.

to the Father is unique and unqualified, so that we might partake, not in a Platonic ideal humanity, but in his "inclusive humanity."[53]

One may think that loving "the one and only" is a supreme example of selfless love. Is this not differentiation, no longer living just for oneself? Not according to Kierkegaard. Christianity commands that one love the neighbor; all else is self-love. Jesus makes this plain when he commands not just to love the neighbor, but love the enemy (Matt 5:43–44). This is what it means to be "children of your Father in heaven" (5:45). He concludes, "For if you love those who love you, what reward do you have? Do not even the tax collectors do the same? In addition, if you greet only your brothers and sisters, what more are you doing than others? Do not even the Gentiles do the same?" (5:46). This is what it means to "be perfect, therefore, as your heavenly Father is perfect" (5:48).

Love Your Enemies?

Whereas the idea of the imitation of God (and of Christ) is present here (cf. Eph 5:1–2), the difficulty of loving one's enemies is all too obvious. The quandary of whether or not this is pertinent to both private and public life has profound implications for social ethics.[54] Perhaps not as an answer but as a new perspective is to see the command as a command of the One who loved his "enemies" (see Rom 5:10; Luke 23:44). Indeed, can we say that he loved *our* enemies *for* us and on our behalf? The burden is not to make love of enemies a panacea to world change (see Moltmann) or to be an impossible ideal that tends to make Christianity irrelevant to the public sphere.[55] The gospel is not to be "used" for the agendas of social change or status quo. Note how Jesus appeals to becoming sons and daughters of the heavenly Father, because he is *the* Son, the vicarious basis for the entirety of Christian existence. One is not simply to obey an abstract law, but to imitate the grace of the Father, who is generous to both the good and the evil; "for he makes his sun rise on the evil and on the good, and sends rain on the righteous and on the unrighteous" (Matt 5:45). We know we are not to be partial in love. "Christian love teaches us to love all people,

---

53. J. B. Torrance, "The Vicarious Humanity of Christ," 140.

54. Allison, *Sermon on the Mount*, 103.

55. Moltmann, *The Way of Jesus Christ*, 130. See the critique by Allison, *Sermon on the Mount*, 101.

The Problem with "Preferential Love"

unconditionally all."[56] Yet only Jesus can love our enemies when we are not able. We can then participate in love, albeit sometimes a difficult journey. However, the focus is on Christ and neither deifying an abstract principle of non-retaliation nor ignoring the presence of Christ in both private and public spheres.

For Kierkegaard, the love that is an imitation of God's grace is far from a self-love that can reflect, for example, love in "the one and only."[57] This devotion to the beloved only creates an obliteration between the two, an "other I," so that love remains only a self-love.[58] Passion is the source of this love, not obedience to the command of neighbor love. The object of love has been chosen.[59] Differentiation within the Trinity brings God beyond simply self-love (see chapter two).

Certainly, the Father is gracious to the Son in the event of the incarnation, through the election of the Son. Yet, as we have seen, the very motivation of the incarnate event was for others. "God so loved the world . . ." (John 3:16). And the love between the Father and the Son in the Spirit certainly did not create an obliteration between the Three Persons of the Trinity. Distinctions between the Father, the Son, and the Holy Spirit matter, avoiding only a being of self-love. The early church saw the importance of this biblical portrait in the entire development of the Trinity: One God, Three Persons. It is important that the Son genuinely prays to the Father, for our sake. That is the salvific meaning of the unique priesthood of Christ (Heb 7:24–25). Even in Paul's doctrine of union with Christ, even being "crucified with Christ" so "it is no longer I who live but it is Christ who lives in me," the individual is never obliterated by Christ. Paul hastens to add, "And the life *I* now live in the flesh *I* live by the faith of (or in) the Son of God" (Gal 2:19–20). The "no longer I who live" somehow means as well "I live by the faith of the Son of God," or, as in other translations, "I live in the Son of God." Note the translation possibility of living not just "in" the Son of God, but by "faith of" the Son of God, the vicarious faith of Christ. The danger of self-love, additionally, of loving only one person exclusively, to the exclusion of others is mitigated by the Son's ability to be devoted

---

56. Kierkegaard, *Works of Love*, 49.
57. Kierkegaard, *Works of Love*, 54.
58. Kierkegaard, *Works of Love*, 54.
59. Kierkegaard, *Works of Love*, 55.

completely to the Father's will and yet be the Son of God "who loved me and gave himself for me" (Gal 2:20), along with the world (John 3:16).⁶⁰

Does not the Son's exclusive bond to the Father also speak of the importance of a particular concrete love that then can be the basis for the love of many? The evangelist may cry to the crowd, "I love you all," but understandably receive a great deal of cynicism. "How can he say he loves me? He doesn't even know me," one can respond. The Son knows and loves the Father, as the Father knows the Son (Matt 11:25–27), so that we can hear the Son's call to us, "Come to me, all you that are weary and are carrying heavy burdens, and I will give you rest" (11:28).

Love and Self-Denial

For Kierkegaard, all erotic and friendship love is preferential, therefore self-love, is in contrast with divine love. However, this does not mean that every natural form is wrong. It simply is not Christian love.⁶¹ For Kierkegaard, the opposite of self-love is self-denial, "which is Christianity's essential form," which connects one with eternity.⁶² Self-esteem is also countered by self-denial, even when one has a "one and only love," because union with that "other I" only creates "a new selfish self." "Self-denial," Kierkegaard believes, "is Christianity's essential form."⁶³

Calvin's denunciation of self-esteem seems off putting to modern ears. However, self-esteem is the opposite of self-denial for the Genevan reformer. For John Calvin, self-denial is "the sum of the Christian life."⁶⁴ (I remember being among the devotees of the sixties' "Marvel Comics" who wrote in feverishly for membership into "The Merry Marvel Marching Society" in order to obtain the button that proudly proclaimed, "I Belong to the Merry Marvel Marching Society!" The need to belong is that primeval!) At its heart is that we "belong to God," no one and nothing else. Rather than being simply a negative state or decision, however, denying self-esteem, self-denial is the reflection of a positive "belonging." The beautiful refrain of "we are not our own" by Calvin, particularly lyrical in his *Golden Booklet of the True Christian Life*, could speak loudly of the basis for a constructive

---

60. Kierkegaard, *Works of Love*, 54–55.
61. Wolterstorff, *Justice in Love*, 112.
62. Kierkegaard, *Works of Love*, 56.
63. Kierkegaard, *Works of Love*, 56.
64. Calvin, *Institutes*, 3.7.1.

The Problem with "Preferential Love"

self-esteem.[65] The substitutionary and vicarious aspect of this should not be missed. We belong because someone has taken our place in death and despair in his vicarious humanity. To belong means that "we are not our own," someone stands in for us.[66] "Reason" and "our will" are not to guide us, but instead "in so far as we can, let us therefore forget ourselves and all that is ours." Our own natural judgment and reason needs be to renounced, because someone has taken our place.[67] "What is your only comfort in life and death?" asks the Heidelberg Catechism, and responds, "That I belong—body and soul—in life and in death—not to myself but to my faithful Savior, Jesus Christ" (Q. 1). Karl Barth adds that the statement "we belong to Jesus Christ" is more important than morality or religion.[68] "Self-denial" for Calvin means "the radical nature of the negative aspect of the Christian life . . . that the self should really be slain, done to death in violence as Christ was done to death."[69] Lloyd Ogilvie, the celebrated preacher of an earlier generation, recalled in an early sermon at Hollywood Presbyterian Church a latter day student of John Calvin, T. F. Torrance, pointing to him in a dark Edinburgh classroom, and saying, "Ogilvie, you must die!" We have been put to death, so the old self is no more and should be forgotten. This "forgetting" is only possible because our identity is in Someone else. Since the basis is the resurrection (making alive . . . *vivification*) as well as the death (putting to death . . . *mortification*) (see Romans 6), self-denial is more than just a negative concept.[70] Indeed, as Charles Partee points out, Calvin uses "self-denial" to say in effect that "we deal with God in everything."[71]

One has already denied himself for us. Christ calls us to deny ourselves because he has denied himself for us. The burden is not on our capability to deny ourselves, as in some traditions of spirituality. T. F. Torrance reminds us that true scientific thinking means that we must be brought under control, "we cannot divorce our questions from ourselves who ask them, for we are part of the questions we ask."[72] That is why Jesus Christ is essential to us, to set us free from ourselves, taking our place, so that we might share

---

65. Calvin, *Institutes*, 3.7.1; Calvin, *Golden Booklet*, 26.
66. Calvin, *Institutes*, 3.7.1; Calvin. *Golden Booklet*, 26.
67. Wallace, *Calvin's Doctrine*, 59.
68. Barth, *Dogmatics in Outline*, 91.
69. Wallace, *Calvin's Doctrine*, 62.
70. Leith, *John Calvin's Doctrine*, 77.
71. Partee, *Theology of Calvin*, 218.
72. T. F. Torrance, *God and Rationality*, 54.

in his life. One cannot hold fast to God, one cannot love God, Kierkegaard contends, unless one admits one's inability. That is what self-denial is all about.[73] Again, the Dane exhorts his readers to admit how little they know about love; they must come to know "the deeper love from God."[74] "Oh, if a human being could in self-denial properly get rid of all illusion, as if he were capable of something . . ." he could wonderfully speak of the love of God.[75] The challenge is to love God truly. Who among us really does that? We should respond christologically; this is why we need the vicarious love of Christ.

Kierkegaard even has a poignant counterpart to the vicarious love of Christ when he speaks of the "reciprocal love" of loving in response by recollecting one who is dead, as well as the parents who unconditionally love their children.[76] They are both "nonbeings," who whether they have loved or not, have been before us, yet cannot pay us back, so there is the opportunity for an unselfish response of love, not expecting anything in return. Quite like the free love of the Son to the Father, this Son denies himself for our sake in his vicarious life, death, resurrection. What is different, of course, is that the Father first loves the Son. Yet the importance of a reciprocal love is there in the vicarious response of Christ, as well as in Kierkegaard's examples. Both are examples of "the freest love."[77]

Self-denial for Calvin has powerful implications for the love of neighbor. Instead of flattering oneself, "a kind of kingdom in his breast," renouncing oneself leaves a place for the love that is patient and kind (1 Cor 13:4–5), the love that "does not seek its own."[78] In terms of the vicarious humanity of Christ, we may say that a radical view of substitutionary atonement does not leave a place for one to seek one's own. The proper place of self-esteem, while not emphasized by Calvin, may be seen in the "as yourself" of "love your neighbor as yourself." Yet, the kingdom of love is different from the "kingdom in his (one's) breast."

---

73. Kierkegaard, *Works of Love*, 363–64.
74. Kierkegaard, *Works of Love*, 364.
75. Kierkegaard, *Works of Love*, 365.
76. Kierkegaard, *Works of Love*, 349.
77. Kierkegaard, *Works of Love*, 351.
78. Calvin, *Institutes*, 3.7.4–5.

The Problem with "Preferential Love"

Erotic and Friendship Love Thrust from the Throne

Kierkegaard does not like to say that neighbor love "displaces" erotic love and friendship, yet he is not hesitant to proclaim that "Christianity has thrust erotic love and friendship from the throne, the love based on drives and inclination, preferential love, in order to place the spirit's love [*Kjerlighed*] in its stead, love for the neighbor . . ."[79] What does it mean for erotic love and friendship to be "thrust . . . from the throne"? Such a "throne" for *eros* creates the other person as simply a sexual object, such as when we say a man stalking a woman "wants a woman." "Strictly speaking, a woman is just what he does not want."[80] Such total commitment that *eros* demands speaks of the need for the vicarious humanity of Christ to take the place completely of a humanity that can so easily become delusioned and obsessed by *eros*. As sad as it is, it is no surprise that Christendom has often overemphasized the problem of *eros*. However, it should not underemphasize it either.

Kierkegaard goes on to say that both erotic love and friendship are related to passion, the passion that exclusively loves one and one only.[81] This is in contrast to neighbor love. The neighbor love that is self-denial possesses a "boundlessness" of love, not meaning to exclude a single one.[82] One might say that Kierkegaard is speaking of a "vicarious" function of neighbor love in regards to preferential love: it takes its place, "in its stead." Including the vicarious humanity of Christ, and his love for the Father, this love can involve an "exclusiveness" in the Son's unique love for the Father, but which issues forth also in a love for many, the One for the Many. The Son's uniqueness does not preclude and may even be the foundation for inclusiveness. Certainly there is a drama here that can seem threatening to erotic and friendship love, as well as to our postmodern, pluralistic society, but is it more threatening than any particular incursion of the substitutionary atonement on our lives?

Does Kierkegaard, however, leave any place for loving "the beloved," with erotic love or friendship? He refuses to see Christianity simply as something "higher" than other loves. This is only "a meddlesome way to ingratiate it (Christianity) with the human craving for knowledge or

---

79. Kierkegaard, *Works of Love*, 44.
80. C. S. Lewis, *The Four Loves*, 135.
81. Kierkegaard, *Works of Love*, 45.
82. Kierkegaard, *Works of Love*, 52.

curiosity."[83] Christianity advocates love for all, a love for the neighbor in equality.[84] However, if one is to love all, this includes the beloved. One does not give up love for the beloved in order to love the neighbor, for the beloved is a neighbor as well.[85] The beloved is a subset of the larger group of loved ones. Karl Barth and Ray Anderson provide perspectives that both embrace and delimit *eros*, especially in terms of physical desire. Anderson frankly admits the "this-worldliness" of the book of Ecclesiastes.[86] If Qoheleth exhorts one to "enjoy life with the wife whom you love," he also recognizes "all the days of your vain life" (Eccl 9:9; cf 1:1–18; 5:18–20). Boredom is bound to seep into any relationship. This is only to recognize that we are seeking something else that sensuality cannot satisfy.[87] For Barth, there is no need to reject true *eros*, where desire is legitimate, when it is "preceded by self-giving and thus controlled, not by the need of the other, but by the joy of being his and of willing to belong to him, the confidence of being well-placed with him, the willingness to make common cause with him."[88] This is different from "blind surrender to the other."

In terms of the vicarious humanity of Christ, we might say that the inclusive love of the Son in the Spirit, based on his exclusive love of the Father, has no need to abandon love as desire, even *eros,* for the Father. Ecclesiologically speaking, it would be similar to abandoning the spiritual life of devotion for God for the sake of the social action or evangelistic ministries of the church, or vice versa. This would be wrong, although, of course, because it has been and is being done in the history of Christianity.

Kierkegaard also claims that it is no good to claim that one can have Christian love "in addition" to praising erotic love and friendship.[89] There is no place for competing deities. The lovers think that their love is the highest but that is not the case because their love lacks the eternal.[90] The "longings" (*Sehnsucht*) that one may have through nature have limitation. Many forget that C. S. Lewis also taught, "Nature does not teach."[91] Erotic

---

83. Kierkegaard, *Works of Love*, 57.
84. Kierkegaard, *Works of Love*, 60.
85. Kierkegaard, *Works of Love*, 61.
86. Anderson, *Exploration into God: Sermonic Meditations on the Book of Ecclesiastes*.
87. Anderson, *Exploration into God: Sermonic Meditations on the Book of Ecclesiastes*.
88. Barth, *CD* III/4, 219.
89. Kierkegaard, *Works of Love*, 45.
90. Kierkegaard, *Works of Love*, 61.
91. C. S. Lewis, *The Four Loves*, 37.

The Problem with "Preferential Love"

love and friendship are not abandoned, however, by "the royal Law" to "love your neighbor as yourself." "Just as this commandment will teach everyone how to love oneself, so it also will teach erotic love and friendship genuine love: in loving yourself, preserve love for the neighbor; in erotic love and friendship, preserve love for the neighbor."[92] There is no dualism in Kierkegaard's understanding of love for the neighbor and the beloved. The love of the lovers can be affected and changed by neighbor love, but it does not have to be obliterated. Certainly, between the Father and the Son there is love that continues even as "God's love has been poured into our hearts through the Holy Spirit that has been given to us" (Rom 5:5). Love for the neighbor becomes the "sanctifying element" in erotic love and friendship, in which a "kinship with God" is developed, based on "humanity's likeness to God," a likeness that is only learned when one loves your neighbor, like God does, not just your preferences, thereby you become "like God."[93]

One might pause when one reads in Kierkegaard "like God." Was it not the temptation in the garden (at least the serpent's interpretation of it) that to eat of the fruit of the knowledge of good and evil would be to be "like God" (Gen 3:5)?[94]

While erotic love and friendship might seem to be selfless, even Christian, because of their devotion, for Kierkegaard they are only reflections again of self-love.[95] "The one and only" of erotic love merges with the self into "the other I, the other self."[96] This merging takes place in the "intoxication" with the beloved and therefore uniting the two in a creation of "a new selfish self."[97] One might see Kierkegaard finding it impossible to distinguish, as C. S. Lewis does, between "gift-love" and "need-love."[98] But that is not the case. One might expect Kierkegaard to say that a need has been fulfilled, but at the expense of cutting oneself off from all others except the beloved. For Kierkegaard, neighbor love is the love that is not preferential, but embraces everyone. The beloved is loved with unrestricted devotion it seems, what could be seen as loving the beloved "as yourself."

---

92. Kierkegaard, *Works of Love*, 62.
93. Kierkegaard, *Works of Love*, 62–63.
94. See Dietrich Bonhoeffer's exposition of Gen 3:5 in *"Sicut Deus,"* in *Creation and Fall*, 111–14.
95. Kierkegaard, *Works of Love*, 57.
96. Kierkegaard, *Works of Love*, 54.
97. Kierkegaard, *Works of Love*, 56.
98. C. S. Lewis, *The Four Loves*, 11ff.; Cf. Smedes, *Mere Morality*, 45ff.

However, it is not. What one loves is not the neighbor but "the other I," not "the first you."[99] The selfishness in preferential love is rooted out by loving the neighbor.[100]

A Need for Love?

Indeed, the "need" for love can be connected with the duty, the "shall" of the commandment. This is a hallmark of Kierkegaard's thought. There is a need to fulfill the duty. We question, however, whether this really upholds the freedom of God. Wolterstorff does not see any relevance to any motives for love: attachment, solidarity, or duty.[101] He will admit that one does one's duty as a "fall back." He seems right in observing that a clarity of motives is not necessary love (*contra* Kant). Yet he will admit that the Samaritan was motivated by compassion. Where does this compassion come from? Wolterstorff appeals to a kind of "disposition" in all human beings. However, is this adequate to depend on such a "disposition" that the bloody history of the human race seems often not to reflect? In the end, Wolterstorff seems to be left with the same naked moral exhortation to love, and simply trying to obey Jesus' commands. If this is all there was, however, would there be a need for a cross and a resurrection?

Kierkegaard finds the difference from preferential love and divine love in the contrast between a love of this world and eternity. Erotic and friendship love are liable to jealous. The proper place for "need-love" of duty is the love that is based in eternity. The "need" in the free person is indeed the true expression of freedom. The one in whom love is a need certainly feels free in his love, and the very one who feels totally dependent, so that he would lose everything by losing the beloved, is not free: "Spontaneous love makes a person free and at the next moment dependent."[102] What is missing in "worldly wisdom" that Christianity teaches is that "love is a relationship between: a person-God-a person, that is, God is the middle term," however "beautiful" a relationship between two people is.[103] Without God, this is a "defraudation" of love, but not to the exclusion of love of self. This is a true love of self: "To love God is to love oneself truly; to help another person to

---

99. Kierkegaard, *Works of Love*, 57.
100. Kierkegaard, *Works of Love*, 44.
101. Wolterstorff, *Justice in Love*, 116–17.
102. Kierkegaard, *Works of Love*, 38.
103. Kierkegaard, *Works of Love*, 106–7.

The Problem with "Preferential Love"

love God is to love another person; to be helped by another person to love God is to be loved."[104] Love is devotion and sacrifice, but only God is able to judge what is truly devotion and sacrifice.[105]

How is God to be "the middle term," however? Is he the God who in an eternal relationship in himself, exists in the response of the Son to the Father on our behalf? Is he the only One who truly helps another person to love God through his love of the Father? The world may see "true love" as "lovelessness."[106] The Father sending the Son to the cross has often been viewed that way. Yet it ends up being the act of greatest love for humanity. That the Son is *homoousios* (same essence) with the Father (Nicaea) means that we have a genuine expression of self-love in God himself, a love that exists from all eternity. That is what the Trinity means.

This misunderstanding of the love the Father has for the Son he sends to the cross is reflected in the misunderstanding of Jesus' teaching to "hate" one's father and mother in order to be a "disciple" of Jesus' (Luke 14:26).[107] Such hyperbole only makes sense in thinking about the faith and obedience of the Son for our sakes, vicarious faith and obedience, as an act of both God and the human. The Son's response of love to the Father on our behalf is not to be considered a condition of the Father's love, but rather as an expression of it.

"Need-Love" and God

One can see the Dane's argument about need in love but still can find it very difficult to follow him at this point. Does the tyranny of an exclusive or primarily "need-love" reflect the divine nature? God does not "need" to love us. He is love in himself from all eternity in the eternal relationship between the Father and the Son through the Spirit. The actions of grace reveal this love. He freely loves in the sense that he does not have to love, and certainly not to love out of duty. Commands, such as the commands to love God and your neighbor, are not necessarily duties. There is a necessity behind a duty or obligation that God's command does not entail. He does not have a "need" to command us. Indeed, the freedom of God to love

---

104. Kierkegaard, *Works of Love*, 107.
105. Kierkegaard, *Works of Love*, 107.
106. Kierkegaard, *Works of Love*, 107.
107. Kierkegaard, *Works of Love*, 108.

is based on God not "needing" to love us.[108] Perhaps we can say that we "need" to obey his commands. "The fulfillment of the commandment to love God is also decided."[109] We reply to this love. However, even that need is not be seen as coerced by God. He does not coerce us to obey. God's commands are given ("gift-love") by the free God and, yes, they are commands, but they are commands that are to be obeyed freely, out of desire, self-giving, and belonging.[110] We "need" his "gift." God addresses that need by saying, "Come unto me . . ."[111] However, they have the kind of freedom that is not libertarian nor the autonomous human action of making a decision between two choices. Rather that kind of freedom can be (to use the philosophical language) "compatibilist" with divine grace and human will, especially when it is centered in Christ, the One who demonstrates what it truly means to be both free and obedient.[112] The "need-love" is defined by the prior self-giving of "gift-love" (Barth). Perhaps "need-love" and "gift-love" come together in the *belonging* between the Father and the Son in the Spirit. The Father and the Son "need" each other but in terms of what T. F. Torrance calls "onto-relations," relations that reflect the relations within the being of the eternal triune God.[113] Torrance is also helpful with his idea of *contingence*.[114] Is there not a contingent (neither necessary nor by chance) relation in the Trinity? There is not a "causal" connection between the Father's and the Son's love.[115] This belonging is not a demonic, possessive one, as in abusive relationships. Rather, it is a reflection of the *perichoresis*, the mutual indwelling of love between the Father and the Son in the Spirit.[116] Here is the basis of the self-giving ("gift-love") between the Father and the Son, made manifest in the incarnation, a belonging that is free, not coercive nor possessive. This love is free, in contrast to the God of

---

108. Barth, *CD* I/1, second ed., 139.
109. Barth, *CD* I/2, 384.
110. Barth, *CD* III/4, 219.
111. C. S. Lewis, *The Four Loves*, 14.
112. For libertarian versus compatibilist freedom, see Sanders, *The God Who Risks*, 36, 218–19; Helm, *Providence of God*, 42–43, and Kettler, "Providence, Evil, Suffering, and the God Who Believes" in *The God Who Believes: Faith, Doubt, and the Vicarious Humanity of Christ*, 132–65.
113. T. F. Torrance, *Mediation of Christ*, 47.
114. T. F. Torrance, *Divine and Contingent Order*, vii.
115. T. F. Torrance, *Mediation of Christ*, 48.
116. T. F. Torrance, *Christian Doctrine of God*, 102–3.

The Problem with "Preferential Love"

Job's friends, as Barth observes.[117] Their God never acts freely, out of grace, but as an automatic "effect" to the "cause" of human sin, which the friends then have to conclude lies hidden with Job. Reward and punishment are the only categories of response for this God. There is no opportunity for "gift-love." Paul Fiddes suggests that God is free to become in need. This is the significance of the *kenosis* (self-emptying) of the Son.[118]

The Freedom of God and "Need-Love"

When the freedom of God is lacking, one's own definition of love for the beloved can easily degenerate into possession. Belonging to God lessens the need to possess someone else, and therefore equate love with obsession and possession.[119] One might think that one needs God's help to love the neighbor, but one can get along very well by oneself in erotic or friendship love.[120] Quite the contrary, without loving and being loved by God first, as seen between the Father and the Son, we teeter closer and closer to love as obsession and possession, that which we do not see between the Father and the Son. The vicarious humanity of Christ intervenes by smashing the idols of obsession and possession deep within our human selves. Unlike the iconoclasm of violence, the vicarious humanity of Christ smashes idols with love. As the early Karl Barth said, "Love, because it sets up no idol, is the demolition of every idol. Love is the destruction of every idol. Love is the destruction of anything that is—*like God*."[121] Unlike the parochial limitations of erotic and friendship love, the love of God can permeate "everything," but that also means changing yet maintaining erotic and friendship love.[122]

---

117. Barth, *CD* IV/3.1, 460.

118. Fiddes, *Participation in God*, 214. I have changed my view on this point in Fiddes's thought since *The God Who Believes: Faith, Doubt, and the Vicarious Humanity of Christ*, 117 n. 126. God's ability to become in "need" certainly, however, radically challenges any belief in a necessity within God as well as God being conditioned by externals. Cf. Anderson, *Historical Transcendence and the Reality of God* on the ability of the transcendence of God to become human.

119. Kierkegaard, *Works of Love*, 107–8.

120. Kierkegaard, *Works of Love*, 112.

121. Barth, *The Epistle to the Romans*, 496.

122. Kierkegaard, *Works of Love*, 112.

CHAPTER TWO

Can Self-Love Be True Love?

The Love of the Self Presupposed?

We have seen that Kierkegaard seeks to maintain a tricky balance between arguing for the limitations of speaking of self-love as true love yet accepting its validity nonetheless as long as it is changed by loving the neighbor. Is there anything, however, left for self-love?

Clearly, Moses and Jesus do not prohibit self-love, whatever they mean by loving your neighbor as yourself.[1] They obviously do not mean to love one's neighbor *instead of* oneself; replacing love of oneself with love of the neighbor is not mentioned.

Yet how can we promote something that is not promoted by Jesus or Scripture and seems to be the opposite of Jesus' call to "self-denial"? Love of neighbor, in fact, is a judgement on my self-love.[2]

Much is made of developing a positive "self-image" today. Many are said to have grown up with damaged self-images. Yet others do not want us to speak very loudly about self-love. Self-love is assumed, says Karl Barth, but he does not want us to "blow on this fire."[3] It "is bright enough already." Self-love is assumed (Mark 12:29–31: Matt 22:37–40; Luke 10:27–28), but there is no *commandment* to do this. However, is this a distinction without a difference? Barth does not think, however, that the mention of self-love,

---

1. Wolterstorff, *Justice in Love*, 97.
2. Barth, *CD* I/2, 387ff, 450ff.
3. Barth, *CD* I/2, 388.

Can Self-Love Be True Love?

is a divine endorsement, or makes it "normal," especially in relation to love of neighbor.[4] Self-love may be "visible" and "tangible," but this is only an indication of love for the neighbor and judgment upon self-love! The loneliness of self-love is a good indicator. "When I love my neighbor I confess that my self-love is not a good thing, that it is not love at all. I begin to love at all only when I love my neighbor."[5] Strong words indeed. Is there any future then for self-love?

One may protest and say that one cannot live without the beloved, but the real test, Kierkegaard argues, is its fruit. Love is known by its fruit.[6] The fruit is found in truth. Is there any truth in that love? Love that lacks "eternity's truth" is really self-love. The Dane recognizes that in the command, "You shall love your neighbor as yourself" (Matt 22:39), the love of the self is presupposed.[7] Yet this is not so because, as is commonly thought, self-love is the love closest to oneself. This does not mean that Christianity views self-love as a "prescriptive right," but as determined "to wrest self-love away from us human beings."

Can Kierkegaard have it both ways, to presuppose self-love and to aim to "wrest" it away?

Common today as much as in Kierkegaard's day, is the belief that love is whatever two persons decide it is.[8] They say they are in love. Nothing more needs to be said; to say otherwise would be judgmental. However, is this not just an expression of the modern axiomatic belief in human autonomy? Yes, to love God is to love oneself truly, for God loves our selves. Loving another person is to help them to love God.[9] The one who is loved, the beloved, decides how the lover should love. However, even this object of love does not know what to judge correctly, what it means to be loved in the sense of being loved by God, nor does the lover know what it means to enable someone to love God.[10] Only someone who already belongs to God knows what it means to love and be loved through God.[11] This is where the God who loves and is loved comes in, in the vicarious humanity

---

4. Barth, *CD* I/2, 450.
5. Barth, *CD* I/2, 450.
6. Kierkegaard, *Works of Love*, 7.
7. Kierkegaard, *Works of Love*, 17.
8. Kierkegaard, *Works of Love*, 106–7.
9. Kierkegaard, *Works of Love*, 107.
10. Kierkegaard, *Works of Love*, 107.
11. Kierkegaard, *Works of Love*, 108.

of Christ. Jesus is the only one who can then call upon us to "hate" father, mother, and sister, and in essence one's life (self-denial) in comparison to love for him (Luke 14:26).[12] Only God can "seek his own" and still be love (1 Cor 13:5).[13] He is the foundation for genuine self-love. The world cannot take everything because it cannot give everything. "This can be done only by God, who takes everything, everything, everything—in order to give everything."[14] The doctrine of creation makes it clear that we are creatures of a limit. That limit is not to be bemoaned but to be celebrated.[15] "His very limiting is His special, exalted, rich and glorious giving," Barth memorably states.[16] The victory of the kingdom of God is not just over "the human failure to be image-bearers," as N. T. Wright and countless others proclaim.[17] Human beings are indeed made in the image of God (Gen 1:26), but they are also made of the dust of the ground (Gen 2:7); they have a limit, as Bonhoeffer stresses.[18] Barth makes the alternative clear: "The doctrine of the autonomy of the free creature over against God is simply the theological form of human enmity against God's grace . . ."[19] We can therefore accept the place of misunderstanding in love: the Son was the most misunderstood of all, the one from whom we need to understand love.[20]

Our desire to be accepted by others as the very definition of being loved is often the source of much travail. George Eldon Ladd, an evangelical New Testament scholar who sought "a place at the table" with mainline scholars, despite a life of significant accomplishment among evangelicals, is a case study of how badly things can turn out in personal life when others equate being loved with acceptance.[21] Jesus presents the exact opposite: "He was in the world, and the world came into being through him; yet the world did not know him" (John 1:10). "His own people did not accept him"

---

12. Kierkegaard, *Works of Love*, 108.
13. Kierkegaard, *Works of Love*, 264.
14. Kierkegaard, *Works of Love*, 103.
15. Barth, *CD* III/4, 568.
16. Barth, *CD* III/4, 568.
17. Wright, *The Day the Revolution Began*, 148.
18. Bonhoeffer, *Creation and Fall*, 85–86, 98–99, 118, 144. See on page 86: "God is at once the boundary and the center of our existence."
19. Barth, *CD* II/1, 586.
20. Kierkegaard, *Works of Love*, 110.
21. See D'Elia, *A Place at the Table*.

(John 1:11). Yet this did not affect his rejoicing before the Father in the Holy Spirit (Luke 10:21).

Erotic and Friendship Loves as Self-Love

Both erotic love and friendship for Kierkegaard are versions of self-love, despite the romantic lover's claim that one loves the beloved more than oneself.[22] Erotic love may rhapsodize about passion and self-sacrifice, but in the end has to finish with erotic love, an inescapable self-love, no matter what else has been sacrificed.[23] Erotic love may be "the beautiful dizziness of infinity," yet it is still a preference of the lover, based on his concern for himself, his self-love, just as friendship love is. A friend is always for, never against, one's friend. Even a teacher has to be professionally "against" another, and cannot be called a friend. Karl Barth wistfully observes that between the world wars, the German people had trouble viewing others as friends.[24] All the nations were "against" them. "I need all the friends I can get," Charlie Brown in the *Peanuts* comic strip once said. Aristotle sees friendship as mixed with self-love, since a friend is good for us; Kierkegaard sees it as simply another kind of self-love.[25] Either way, there is the total need for Christ, for Christ to enter in, the only one who truly sacrifices. Christ enters as the unique friend, the friend who exists when we seem not to have a friend, bridging the difference, and calling us friends (John 15:14).

One would think that God's love has a right to be possessive, like a love of a king for his country. However, in Christ the opposite is true. Christ Jesus, for Paul, "though he was in the form of God did not think equality with God a thing to be exploited but emptied himself, taking the form of a slave . . ." (Phil 2:6-7). Heaven "floats around us like a cloud" and is the most real thing we can know, writes Jayber Crow, but we cannot possess it, just as we can never possess another person and call it "love."[26] That remains as self-love. Hell, for Jayber, is the failure of love, "the leftovers of my life; things I might once have done that are now undoable, old wrongs,

---

22. Kierkegaard, *Works of Love*, 18–19.
23. Kierkegaard, *Works of Love*, 273.
24. Barth, *The Only Way*, 92–94, 97.
25. Aristotle, *Nicomachean Ethics*, 1156b 6–11; 1159a 7–10 in *Introduction to Aristotle*, 473–76, 482; Wolterstorff, *Justice in Love*, 111.
26. Berry, *Jayber Crow*, 351.

responsibilities unmet, ineradicable failures—things of time, which is always revealing the remedies it has already carried us beyond . . . where there is such a groaning travail of selfishness in all its forms . . ."[27] Can the love of Jesus for the Father triumph over our failures, however? We can say that though we fail at love, Christ does not. He knows God, and heaven, for us. This is our hope.

The Neighbor and the Self

The key difference in Christian love of the object is not one of preference, but the neighbor, the human being next to oneself, including the enemy. The neighbor, by English etymology, is the "near dweller" (Merriam-Webster). Not only are you "near" to yourself, but also there is "the other" who challenges your selfishness.[28] This "other' teaches us how to love oneself in "the right way."[29] Therefore, self-love is neither excluded nor denied by Kierkegaard.

This neighbor is to be loved "as yourself," but this is not applied to God. Too often, the love of neighbor "as yourself" is separated from the previous exhortation to love the Lord your God with all your strength, etc.[30] There is a distinction in love here between love for God and love for the neighbor.[31] One may be a humanist of any stripe and sees the benefits or obligation to love one's neighbor in the same way that you cannot avoid taking care of yourself. To love one's neighbor is to realize "what an enormous claim God and eternity have upon the individual himself."[32] This contrasts with the "childishness" of "Me wants." This "I" has no significance unless "eternity incessantly speaks and says: *You* shall, *you* shall, *you* shall."

However, neighbor love must reflect 1 Cor 13:5: "love does not seek its own." Yet "mine" and "yours" are by definition relational terms.[33] This brings us back to the relation between the Father and the Son, where a

---

27. Berry, *Jayber Crow*, 354–55.
28. Kierkegaard, *Works of Love*, 21.
29. Kierkegaard, *Works of Love*, 22.
30. Kierkegaard, *Works of Love*, 19.
31. See the argument against the identity between the love of God and the love of neighbor as found in Karl Rahner in Paul Molnar, "Love of God and Love of Neighbor in the Theology of Karl Rahner and Karl Barth," *Modern Theology*.
32. Kierkegaard, *Works of Love*, 90.
33. Kierkegaard, *Works of Love*, 265.

"mine" and a "yours" exists eternally, yet without a seeking of one's own. Self-love can exist within such a reality, where the Son's response to the Father *is truly his own, yet he does not seek his own* (Phil 2:1–11). God's love, *pace* Nygren, is not just "spontaneous," which can be a fleeting feeling, and therefore in contrast to the measurability of justice.[34] God's love implies justice, in terms of giving each his own, as an active part of love, not simply "balancing the scales." It seeks to do the just thing, yet ends up destroying the distinction between "mine" and "yours," the end result of all kinds of socialism.[35] Yet, who among us is wise enough to know what is good for the other? We need "the mind of Christ" (1 Cor 2:16).

Erotic love, however, seeks for a change, an obliteration between "mine" and "yours," so that the two lose their identities in their love.[36] Is not the love between the Father and the Son a critique of such erotic love, or at least of its superiority? The love between the Father and the Son does not need the destruction of the persons, of the "mine" and the "yours." In fact, it avoids the confusion of the erotic lovers by a "mutual indwelling" (*perichoresis*) of love that is genuine sharing yet also differentiation. The obliteration of differentiation in human beings always ends up badly, as the worst of "mind-controlling" religions testify.

Even in this obliteration, however, self-love still shines through. The selves exchanged are still "mine" and "yours."[37] They give up everything except their selves.[38] Erotic love and friendship remain "enhanced and augmented self-love."[39]

Neighbor love can exist within self-love, as seen in an example of "vicarious" love by Kierkegaard. This is the "hiddenness" of help, supremely seen in the vicarious humanity of Christ. He helps us, not to lose our individuality, but to be helped to become our own person. If he could be seen, then we would be slavishly dependent. If I see the other's help then I do not become my own person.[40] God want us to become adults. Yet we totally need his help, to become truly free. Thus, Christ acts in an "unnoticed"

---

34. Nygren, *Agape and Eros*, 75; See also Wolterstorff, *Justice in Love*, 42–43.
35. Kierkegaard, *Works of Love*, 265.
36. Kierkegaard, *Works of Love*, 265–66.
37. Kierkegaard, *Works of Love*, 266.
38. Kierkegaard, *Works of Love*, 273.
39. Kierkegaard, *Works of Love*, 266.
40. Kierkegaard, *Works of Love*, 279.

way.[41] (Echoes of Bonhoeffer's "world come of age" resound here.) Love does not seek its own. The Son does not hand out "Jesus" T-shirts to be worn. He is "God Incognito."[42]

The Command of God and the Hearing of the Son

Christologically, *redoubling* is based on the *kenosis* of God in Jesus Christ. In the incarnation, Jesus "forgets" himself for the sake of others, allowing only God to think of him.[43] However, one must remember that there is one Jesus Christ in whom his divine and human natures "communicate" with one another, the classic doctrine of the *communicatio idiomatum*.[44] This is important in terms of the humanity of Christ. His humanity did not just disappear after the incarnation. He continues to be human in order to intercede for us (Heb 7:25). He is one Jesus Christ, divine and human.

Redoubling maintains the *communicatio idiomatum,* the unity of the divine and the human in Christ. While still reflecting the adverbs of the Council of Chalcedon (AD 451), not to be divided, the two natures of Christ are not to be confused, *indivise et inseparabiliter*.[45] This *redoubling* reminds us of the dynamic action within the divine and human natures of Christ that reflects the dynamic of the eternal Father-Son relationship. In the incarnation, as well as in the eternal Trinity, "the one who loves is or becomes what he does . . . he has or rather he acquires what he gives . . . the one who loves has what he gives."[46] This is done by the one person, the God-man, Jesus Christ. This "redoubling" of love has the power to hide a multitude of sins (1 Pet 4:8). As an outward work, as a work of love, God gives to humanity in Jesus Christ. However, he also, in the vicarious response of Christ, gives back to God, reflecting the inner relations between the Father and the Son.[47] Our place as human beings is now replaced by

---

41. Kierkegaard, *Works of Love*, 274–76.
42. Kierkegaard, *Practice in Christianity*, 127–33.
43. Kierkegaard, *Works of Love*, 281.
44. T. F. Torrance, *Incarnation*, 209; Muller, "*communicatio idiomatum/communicatio/proprietatum*" in *Dictionary of Latin and Greek Theological Terms: Drawn Principally from Protestant Scholastic Theology,* 72–74.
45. T. F. Torrance, *Incarnation*, 208.
46. Kierkegaard, *Works of Love*, 281.
47. See Kierkegaard, *Works of Love*, 282.

the humanity of the Son, since now we realize our incapacity, and the Son's ability, even in self-denial.[48]

If the Son lives in a relationship of continually hearing the word of the Father in faith and obedience, then it is *he* who first hears the "*You shall.*" The command of God in the two greatest commandments is first for Jesus. As Eduard Thurneysen comments on the Sermon on the Mount, "the proclaimer of the new way becomes himself what is proclaimed."[49] He is both the One who commands and the One who is commanded. That is why the Sermon on the Mount cannot be understood apart from the One who is speaking it.[50] A certain kind of Christian moralism can detach Jesus from his own ethical teaching, especially when they become "timeless truths." The connection between the narrative of Jesus and his teaching is always essential. At the heart of that narrative is his faith in, obedience in, and love for the Father.

However, his love for the Father is different, a love that we cannot do. We need the vicarious love of the Son for the Father, love that does not simply love the Father like we love ourselves, as self-love, but is the unique eternal love of the Son for the Father. The second commandment, Jesus says, is "like" the first in that it is also a command to love; however, it is unlike the first, needing both strength of intensity and exclusivity for these loves, for both God and the neighbor, something that is only reserved for God. This is something only the Son can do. Who among us can ever say that they love the Lord their God with all their strength? We need to depend on the mercy of the Son's vicarious faith and obedience.

Yet when that is the case, we see this as a reality in our lives. This reality is found in Kierkegaard's plea to love oneself "in the right way."[51] In fact, the Dane sees the lack of the "right" self-love as the source of suicides. This "right way" is found most profoundly in the love of the neighbor. What is the essence of love of neighbor? For Kierkegaard it is "to help another person to love God." Where is this more manifest then in the life of Jesus himself? His vicarious life and work was to enable humanity to be redeemed in order to be new people that love God (justification and sanctification together). "If you are a nice person—if virtue comes easily to you—beware!" warns C. S.

---

48. Kierkegaard, *Works of Love*, 365.
49. Thurneysen, *Sermon on the Mount*, 13.
50. Thurneysen, *Sermon on the Mount*, 14.
51. Kierkegaard, *Works of Love*, 22.

Lewis.[52] Christianity is not just "improvement but transformation."[53] The transformation is not just formation but, in Bonhoeffer's words, "conformation" to Christ.[54] This is not first something we do. "Love is the reconciliation of man with God in Jesus Christ . . . Love, therefore, is the name for what God does to man in overcoming the disunion in which man lives."[55] In contrast to just trying "to become like Jesus," it is "the form of Jesus Christ itself [that] works upon us in such a manner that it molds our form in its own likeness (Gal 4:19). Christ remains the only giver of forms."[56] The vicarious aspect of this is clear. He actively responds to the *"You shall"* for us and on our behalf. In that, we are conformed to him. To embrace this is truly to love oneself.

Self-love seems in obvious antithesis to self-denial, the denial of self in the discipleship of Jesus. "Self-denial means knowing only Christ, no longer knowing oneself," writes Bonhoeffer.[57] Knowing Christ alone means knowing also his necessary suffering, something self-love abhors.

The perfect hearing of the command of God from the Son is in stark contrast with the one whom Kierkegaard, in inimitable irony, exhorts to "forget" God if you want to be well off, despite the fact that he created you from nothing.[58] You owe him "everything," but "forget" him nonetheless. In contrast is Christ, who wants to become "nothing." You will lose everything (even though you never possessed it in the first place). God is the only one who really gives. The contrast with the obedient, hearing Son of the Father could not be greater.

The hearing of the Son is the second movement in the one act of God in Jesus Christ. This hearing has taken place, not only from all eternity in the relationship between the Father and the Son through the Spirit, but now in time, in the incarnation. Coming into this time, it has genuine time, what Kierkegaard calls *redoubling*, or what we have seen in the double movement of the incarnation; first humanward in the solidarity with all humanity in Jesus Christ, then Godward in the vicarious humanity of Christ. Because there is that second movement as well, Kierkegaard's *redoubling* might be

---

52. C. S. Lewis, *Mere Christianity*, 181.
53. C. S. Lewis, *Mere Christianity*, 183.
54. Bonhoeffer, *Ethics*, 92.
55. Bonhoeffer, *Ethics*, 335–36.
56. Bonhoeffer, *Ethics*, 93.
57. Bonhoeffer, *Discipleship*, 86.
58. Kierkegaard, *Works of Love*, 102.

helpful.[59] In the case of *redoubling,* the first movement is outward, from God to humanity. The second movement, then, is inward, from humanity to God.[60] Here is where the *hearing* of the Son responds to the *command* of God. The basis of the command to serve is that the "original fulfillment" is made by God himself, the One who has assumed the form of a slave (Phil 2:7; John 13:12f; Matt 10:24f).[61] Love is in one moment, the same act with two movements. Love is on both sides, the outward and the inward. The eternal Son becomes human, yet his incarnation is not complete without returning to the Father in perfect faith, obedience, worship, and service. He does so not just for himself, but also for others, vicariously.[62]

Self-Love and the Love for Others

Yet is self-love still self-love if it is love invested in the fate of others? "For the sake of the joy that was set before him (Christ) endured the cross . . . (Heb 12:2). Even Calvin recognizes the place of grief over a lost one: "Nor, in the school of Christ, do we learn any such philosophy as requires us to put off that common humanity with which God has endowed us, that, being human, we should be turned into stones."[63] Self-love, then, can coincide with love for others. In fact, one might see this as a *vicarious* act, weeping on behalf of those who are even emptied of weeping.[64] Christ is the physician who possesses one thing that the patients do not possess: hope.[65] To give up hope is to give up on love.[66] Yes, he can possess the self-love of hope, but for our sakes. Only he is able to do this.

Still, a lack of love may exist among those whom we would think most naturally love each other, such as families. Some of our greatest despairs consist of such failed love. Such emptiness contributes to Ecclesiastes' sadness about life.[67] Longings for others are still our longings. Disappointments with loved ones are our greatest disappointments.

---

59. Kierkegaard, *Works of Love,* 280ff.
60. Kierkegaard, *Works of Love,* 280.
61. Barth, *CD* III/4, 662.
62. Barth, *CD* III/4, 281.
63. Calvin, *Writings on Pastoral Piety,* 300.
64. Kettler, *The God Who Rejoices,* 29–30, 92.
65. Kierkegaard, *Works of Love,* 258–59.
66. Kierkegaard, *Works of Love,* 255.
67. Anderson, *Exploration into God,* 29.

Self-love may be a longing within oneself as well, but also a longing for the reconciliation of all things, not purely selfish, a "despair over the earthly" (Kierkegaard) that is not fulfilled. The cosmological extent of this can transcend the selfish.[68]

---

68. Kettler, *The God Who Rejoices*, 33–36.

CHAPTER THREE

The "Double Love" of God and Neighbor

How Do Love of God and Love of Neighbor Live Together?

We have seen that the second commandment to love your neighbor as yourself is both "like" the first, to *love* the Lord your God, but also "unlike" in that we are to love God with all of our strength, etc., However, to love him *"as yourself,"* as in the second commandment, is missing. What is the "like" then? It means, obviously, that both commands involve love. Beyond that, how do both commands relate to one another?

"Loving God Above All Else..."

Kierkegaard suggests, "only by loving God above all else can one love the neighbor in the other human being."[1] In fact, the neighbor who is the other human being is every existing human being. What does the Dane mean? Michael Polanyi famously argues for community as the foundation of faith: "Our believing is conditioned at its source by our belonging."[2] Perhaps because we cannot literally love every human being, *the neighbor*

---

1. Kierkegaard, *Works of Love*, 57.
2. Polanyi, *Personal Knowledge*, 322.

at hand (vicariously?) represents all others. The neighbor is the *Stellvertreter*, the one of "vicarious representative action," according to Bonhoeffer, who not only acts on behalf of another, but who, in Christine Schliesser's words, "actually takes the very place of the other, one who trades position and situation with another."[3] The reality of "the vicarious" is readily evident in the world, Bonhoeffer observes, in the father, the political leader, the instructor, or the apprentice.[4] However, it is only through Jesus that all of life has become vicarious (no *analogia entis* here): "Through him, therefore, all human life is in essence vicarious representation . . . All that human beings were supposed to live, do, and suffer was fulfilled in him."[5] Because of sin, the human race often resists this calling. However, this not nullify that, because of Jesus, the calling of "vicarious representative action" is the calling to be *responsible*, regardless of whether one heeds the call. The calling is *ex opere operato*. The human being remains responsible for the neighbor, "a father remains a father for good or ill."[6]

Why is love of God imperative for loving the neighbor? Because only God as the origin and source of all (Bonhoeffer) is uniquely able to love one whom we do not know, the neighbor on the road (the parable of the Good Samaritan, Luke 10:25–37). It is crucial to remember who spoke these commandments. Jesus is the source of our knowledge of God. "Is God really like Jesus?" asked the dying soldier on the battlefield to T. F. Torrance when he was an army chaplain.[7] There is no division between Jesus and God. If incarnational language is purely "mythical" than we do not have any knowledge of God, as in John Hick's de-personalization of God into "the Real."[8] Charles Hughes questions Hick on whether one can call the Real a being who loves, if the Real is, in essence, ineffable.[9] The God of Jesus is not distant, but near, near to love the neighbor. The obedience of Christ teaches us, Barth claims, "that for God it is just as natural to be lowly as it is to be high, to be near as it is to be far, to be little as it is to be great, to be abroad as it is to be at home."[10] Therefore, "the One who reconciles the world with

---

3. Schliesser, *Everyone Who Acts Responsibly*, 38–39, n. 5.
4. Bonhoeffer, *Ethics*, 257.
5. Bonhoeffer, *Ethics*, 258.
6. Bonhoeffer, *Ethics*, 259.
7. T. F. Torrance, *Mediation of Christ*, 59.
8. Gillis, *A Question of Final Belief*, 163.
9. Hughes, "Pluralism, Inclusivism, and Christology," 163.
10. Barth, *CD* IV/1, 192.

God is necessarily the one God Himself in His true Godhead. Otherwise the world would not be reconciled with God."[11] Jesus is the source of our faith and obedience. Faith and love need to coexist eventually. The trials and temptations of this life are too common to ignore this, witness any marriage or relation of love. One eventually has to trust, have faith in, the beloved. The love of the neighbor is much harder, when we need the most for the faith of Jesus to coincide with love for the neighbor. Otherwise, love can all too easily evaporate into sentimentality.

Christ loves God above all else, especially seen in the depths of his vicarious humanity, or in Bonhoeffer's word, *Stellvertretung* ("vicarious representative action"). This overcoming of sin includes taking on punishment as well for Bonhoeffer, despite the widespread critics of "penal" atonement today, such as by N. T. Wright.[12] Penal substitution can certainly be presented in a crude way, but Bonhoeffer argues that it is simply taking the consequences of sin seriously, and he calls Luther to his side in agreement with him. This is not simply an ethical move, however, because why should one person bear the punishment for many?

It is a move of what T. F. Torrance will call "the soteriological suspension of the ethics."[13] By this Torrance means that the objective reality of what Christ's active obedient life in the depths of our depravity and that of the cosmos, based on his inner, filial relation to the Father, bears fruit for us in a relationship of a moral life based on grace, not external legal relations in abstract moral or legal principles. The God who gives this gift to us is the God we love, the God of grace.

Loving God and Loving the Neighbor

We know love for the ones we know, the erotic beloved or the friend. We can choose to love them because we have come to know them. Importantly, Kierkegaard argues that it is by "loving God" that we can love the neighbor, not just believing in God, having faith in God, etc. But the neighbor who is not our friend, who is not our relative, who may be even our "enemy," may seem to be impossible to love, despite the command by Jesus (Matt

11. Barth, *CD* IV/1, 193.

12. Bonhoeffer, *Sanctorum Communio*, 155–56; Wright, *The Day the Revolution Began*.

13. T. F. Torrance, "The Atonement, the Singularity of Christ and the Finality of the Cross: The Atonement and the Moral Order," 252; Speidell, *Fully Human in Christ*, 1–37.

22:39; 5:44). The scientists seems to tell us that we are genetically imprinted simply to protect our in-group.[14] Here is where the vicarious love of the Son becomes significant. He loves God. "Here at last is a man who loves the Lord with all his heart and soul and mind and strength and his neighbor as himself," Tom Smail exclaims.[15] If mysticism is an unmediated relation to God, then the mysticism of Christ is the foundation for all human mysticism. We participate in his mysticism. His "Abba" experience, of intimacy and reverence, in spite of the cross, becomes ours (Matt 3:17; 11:25–27; Mark 14:34; Luke 23:46; Rom 8:15; Gal 4:6).[16] The Son's mystical union with the Father provides the motivation for a moral union, the obedience of the Son. Therefore, in him, our mystical union with Christ is the basis for our moral union (James Stewart).[17] This is the moral creativity of love, yet love is more than simply the moral; it is intimacy and inwardness. This intimacy and inwardness says something about the nature of God being far more than just omnipotence and omnipresence. "God *is* dependence rendered infinite," Alan Lewis dares to write, "unable to be Father without the Son, or Son without the Father, just as the Spirit, neither self-generating nor self-regarding, proceeds from the Father of the Son as necessary source, and finds it raison d'être in the glorifying of them both."[18] The Son's dependence on the Father is not extrinsic to the Father's being. T. F. Torrance does not like to see "obedience" in God ontologically, as Barth does, but can he avoid doing so when he says, "Whatever is said of the Father," claims T. F. Torrance, "is said of the Son except Fatherhood, and whatever is said of the Son is said of the Father except Sonship."[19] Does not sonship include dependence in some fashion, but not defined by our limited view which would imply inferiority? The Son does loves the Father in response to the Father's love. The Son defines for himself what his response to the Father is like. He is "the perfect Eucharistic being" (Schmemann).[20] "Eucharist (thanksgiving) is the state of perfect man. Eucharist is the life of paradise. Eucharist is the only full and real response of man to God's creation, redemption and gift of

---

14. Barbour, *Nature, Human Nature, and God*, 57.
15. Smail, "Can One Man Die for the People?," 87.
16. See Kettler, *The God Who Believes*, 74–83.
17. Stewart, *A Man in Christ*, 164–65.
18. A. E. Lewis, *Between Cross and Resurrection*, 414.
19. T. F. Torrance, "The Christian Apprehension of God the Father," 134.
20. Schmemann, *For the Life of the World*, 38.

The "Double Love" of God and Neighbor

heaven. But this perfect man who stands before God is *Christ*.[21] That is the foundation for our love of God.

Yet this involves genuine actions on behalf of the other, as Bonhoeffer hastens to add: "self-renouncing, active work for the neighbor, intercessory prayer; and, finally, the mutual forgiveness of sins."[22] Self-sacrifice cannot be denied here.

Genuine love to God, Barth writes, comes from realizing our incapacity to love: "We have to recognize that He intercedes for us and represents us, that what is our own, even our own love for Him, can never be anything but our shame and our curse."[23] The prayers of Jesus are manifestations of our weakness but also of faith in the Father.[24] This is a witness of God that he is the hearer and answerer of prayer. This confidence in the love of God moves Jesus to prayer, John McLeod Campbell contends. Christ is mediator in that act as well. The fruit that is the neighbor comes from "the One for the sake of the Many," as the concrete representative of the entirety of humanity that God loves. Therefore, the neighbor on the road, the "near" one, as in the Good Samaritan parable, represents all. Love must be concrete, however, not abstract. "The love with which we reply to the love of God for us," writes Barth, "can begin and grow only when we go beyond what we can claim as our own love, when we recognize that we the unloving are beloved by Him."[25] This love is repentance before "the mirror of the Word of God which acquits and blesses us, which is itself the love of God to us."[26]

The object of love, however, will commonly determine what is sacrificial for the lover. The lover (if one wants to stay loved!) will not demand.[27] Yet this depends on whether or not one can judge correctly. Who is to say that one's act of devotion is another's pathetic attempt at arousing pity? Kierkegaard argues loving the other person truly is to help one love God.

This is where the vicarious love of Christ is significant. He loves God. He knows what it means to love God; we do not. In fact, we will most likely view the love of God as lovelessness (see the cross of Jesus). Yet to love God is genuine self-love. What helps one to love God is truly helping the beloved

---

21. Schmemann, *For the Life of the World*, 37–38.
22. Bonhoeffer, *Sanctorum Communio*, 184.
23. Barth, *CD* I/2, 384.
24. Campbell, *The Nature of the Atonement*, 176.
25. Barth, *CD* I/2, 384.
26. Barth, *CD* I/2, 390.
27. Kierkegaard, *Works of Love*, 107.

and therefore is an expression of the lover's self-love. The lover desires the good of the beloved. Still, this dethrones belonging to someone else instead of God. Rather, "unless in the same love he belongs to God and dare not possess anyone in love unless the other and he himself belong to God in this love—a person dare not belong to another as if that other person were everything to him."[28]

Loving one's neighbor reflects the love of God. Therefore, justice is not to be seen as in "tension" with love, but as an expression of God's love. If one loves another, Nicholas Wolterstorff argues, one will seek what is just for that person.[29] This certainly corresponds to God's being in his act of the incarnation; because he is love, he seeks what is just for us. The Son knows that love, so he also seeks that justice. Our problem is that we have skewed views of not only love but also justice, so "love" and "justice" become simply ciphers for whatever we like or do not like. We suffer from an impoverishment of both love and justice. We need someone who knows what love is, the love the Father has for the Son and the Son for the Father, and can exhibit that in his life and ministry, a life and ministry in which love and justice are not bifurcated. During my seminary days there existed a well-meaning group of seminarians called the "Human Concerns Committee." If you asked them, they would say their agenda was "peace and justice," social concerns. In opposition to them was the "Missions Concerns Committee." Love, I guess, was left to the missionaries. However, what was left for both was only one-half of the whole gospel.

How is Neighbor Love "Like" Loving God?

The relationship with God, love for God, therefore is not to be seen as "separate but equal" from the love of neighbor. Love for God is too concrete, too particular, so the way love of neighbor may be "like" love of God (Matt 22:39) in its concreteness, but not in its identity.[30] So also the concreteness of love becomes an imperative to love the brother or sister you see if one is to love God, whom one cannot see (1 John 4:20). However, the reciprocity between God and humanity is not left for humanity to fulfill. Jesus Christ,

---

28. Kierkegaard, *Works of Love*, 107–8.

29. Wolterstorff, *Justice in Love*, 83–84.

30. See the argument against the identity of love of God and love of neighbor as found in Karl Rahner, in Molnar, "Love of God and Love of Neighbor in the Theology of Karl Rahner and Karl Barth," 567–99.

The "Double Love" of God and Neighbor

in his vicarious humanity and love for the Father, has created that reciprocity, providing an emancipation from love seeking its own foundation, and in effect, forsaking a spontaneity of love based on the autonomous existence of the Christian.[31] It does become spontaneous and free when it is emancipated from seeking its own ground. This was the intention of God's election of Israel, to create, in Torrance's words, a "community of reciprocity": "I will be your father and you will be my son."[32] This was certainly part of the challenge for Kierkegaard in speaking of love as duty. However, this is also true when love is simply viewed as an expression of autonomy. Love for God can easily be given its "ghetto" existence, and erotic and friendship loves are left to go their way, as either duty or autonomy. This is increasingly true in postmodern society. Personal autonomy is valued most of all, particularly when it comes to erotic and friendship loves. These are based on our preferences, our choices. (The increasing acceptance of same-sex love comes to mind.) Yet love for the neighbor, Kierkegaard contends, does not deny erotic and friendship loves, but transforms them.[33] The erotic is understood as a "drive" not opposed by Christianity.[34] Any opposition would be found in eating and drinking as well. No, the distinction is in the presence of "spirit" in Christianity. It has to understand the "sensuous" nature as something different, the sensuous as selfishness, another form of unchastened self-love.[35] However, in principle, Christianity is not opposed to erotic and friendship loves. The opposition, ironically, is when society wants God to ignore the significance of these loves, leaving them to get along by themselves, rather than the gospel permeating everything.[36] Beyond Kierkegaard, this becomes particularly evident if we see the Son as the One who first loves both God and the neighbor. The unity of the two is ultimately christological.

---

31. T. F. Torrance, *God and Rationality*, 162–63. Cf. "spontaneous" love as "the most striking feature of God's love as Jesus represents it" in Nygren, *Agape and Eros*, 75.
32. T. F. Torrance, *Mediation of Christ*, 12–13.
33. Kierkegaard, *Works of Love*, 112.
34. Kierkegaard, *Works of Love*, 52.
35. Kierkegaard, *Works of Love*, 53.
36. Kierkegaard, *Works of Love*, 112.

How Is Neighbor Love "Unlike" Loving God?

Love for neighbor is "like" love for God because at least both involve love![37] If human love is "like" divine love, should not human love in some capacity correspond to who God really is? However, the vicarious love of Christ reminds us that we not only do not know God but we also do not know what love truly is. Neighbor love, to some extent, has to be "unlike" the love of God. We see glimmers and reflections through a cracked mirror, just enough to whet our appetites! Such a love cannot simply reflect a view of justice based on conflict situations.[38] Is justice simply another attribute in God that must be viewed on the same plane as love? That seems true to many "theories" of the atonement in the history of theology. The Son's love for the Father that takes the place of our ideas of love, would argue otherwise. God is not eternally facing conflict situations in his triune being. The Son's obedient response to the Father concurs with that. In addition, justice is that which flows from the love in God's being; it has its source, its motivation, in the love of God's being, but it cannot be valued as an ontological partner with love. Justice is a derivative of love, not an equal partner. Wolterstorff comes close to saying this when he states that I can treat you justly, give what you deserve, without any conflict between us. That is because I value your worth.[39] Is not this the biblical testimony of the life between the Father and the Son through the Spirit that exists from all eternity? Is this not what we then see in the life of the faithful, obedient, loving Son who on earth and then in heaven continually responds to the love of the Father, a response that is then done on our behalf and in our place? However, some understandings of the atonement may differ with this, if they view a conflict between the wrathful Father appeased by the blood of the innocent Son in the death of Jesus.

Forgiveness, then, may violate justice, as Anselm claims (*Proslogion* 8), hence for him the problem of the atonement and the need for God's honor to be satisfied.[40] "Moral seriousness," Wolterstorff adds, would never allow one to forgive someone who is unwilling to confess the wrong or is dead.[41] Yet is not our love "like" God's when we are exhorted to forgive

---

37. Wolterstorff, *Justice in Love*, 90.
38. Wolterstorff, *Justice in Love*, 90.
39. Wolterstorff, *Justice in Love*, 90.
40. Anselm, *Prologion* 8.
41. Wolterstorff, *Justice in Love*, 173.

The "Double Love" of God and Neighbor

seventy-times seven, without any conditions (Matt 18:21–22)? It is like the God and Father of the Lord Jesus Christ, certainly, whose atonement is not to meet any conditions so that God may love, but to act in accordance with his being of God for us and in our place, in the entirety of the life, death, and resurrection of the faithful and obedient Son. Such a forgiveness may violate a definition of justice which is purely Aristotelian, that we get what we deserve. In the atonement of Christ we do get, however, what we *need*, deliverance from sin and death and union with the risen life of Jesus. God does not give us what we deserve, which is simply the way of sin and death, the way humanity goes without, when he gives us up to our own devices (Rom 1:24–32).

In other words, God's love is not rooted in a conflict in the triune life of God, but it is able, nonetheless, to deal with conflict, the conflict first between God and humanity. Nygren's classic agapism demands treatment for everyone always with agape love.[42] Reinhold Niebuhr, however, adds that the historical situation of this present age includes all sorts of competing values, creating a tragic situation that love cannot handle.[43] Otherwise, victimization will lead to annihilation. (Thus, the need for "just war" theory.) Love may be the eschatological reality; but for now, we seek for some kind of justice. The love that does not seek its own can only fall victim to others.

Reinhold Niebuhr is undoubtedly correct in acknowledging the forces of this world.[44] However, is that not the reason we need Christ to take our place and live a life that finds victory in his falling as victim? It is true that simply trying to be "like Jesus" is foolish. He is the only One who can do that which means salvation. We live in the tragic world of Niebuhr. This is a world of tragedy because of the conflict between self-interested parties. However, we must not ignore the reality of his vicarious life, death, and resurrection, for us. Our neighbor love will always be imperfect, in that way, "unlike" the love of Jesus. However, his love is sufficient. It is enough. We seek to be conformed to him. In addition, even in the historical realities, that is good. Not exhaustive, but good.

---

42. Wolterstorff, *Justice in Love*, 50.
43. Wolterstorff, *Justice in Love*, 65.
44. Niebuhr, *Nature and Destiny of Man*, Vol. 2, 72. Cf. Wolterstorff, *Justice in Love*, 65. See Wood, *The Comedy of Redemption* on the limits of tragedy in Niebuhr, 4–22. See Anderson on the tragic in homosexuality in "Homosexuality: Theological and Pastoral Considerations," 266–83 and *Something Old, Something New*, 143.

The God Who Loves and Is Loved

The atonement means that Jesus loves the Father perfectly, for us and in our place. In contrast to the possibility of human love as subject to lack or loss, this love is never possibly "tragic." We need such a love. The neighbor love Jesus commands is "like" the command to love God only because it is based and grounded on the Father's love for the Son and the Son's love for the Father, a non-tragic love. However, how does that become our own? Sacrificial love can be a tragic whim, accomplishing nothing and probably creating more evil, such, as Niebuhr points out, victimization. This is not true of a love grounded in the love of the Father for the Son, a love that participates in the triune God's continual love, including that very human love of the Son for the Father, a love qualitatively "unlike" our own. The question for us then is, Where in the world or in our daily existence does the triune God actively love? That is where we should be. That is the *locus* of the atonement. In contrast to Niebuhr, it is irrelevant whether we see the good effects. We may never. As John Howard Yoder famously puts it, we are not called to be successful, but to be obedient. In addition, I would add, by participating in the continual obedient love of the Son through the Spirit.

Niebuhr believes that love should be left for the eschaton and we should center on a justice that, nonetheless, involves coercion, if not violence.[45] Here Niebuhr seems to assume naively that the state can always seek for justice. No, it, too, has a self-interest in its preservation that clashes with doing the just act. He is right, however, that love does not involve coercion. The witness of the Gospels is that Jesus went to the cross, despite its horror, willingly (Matt 26:36–46; Mark 14:32–42; Luke 22:40–46). He was not forced by the Father to go to the cross. By separating love (not coercive) from justice (coercive), Niebuhr separated justice from love. Is not this different if justice flows from love, the trinitarian love of the Father, the Son, and the Holy Spirit? Wolterstorff adds that although justice is not based on conflict he does not give the trinitarian foundation for this.[46] In contrast to Niebuhr, Wolterstorff wants both love and justice in the present age because "love incorporates justice."[47] However, does this mean that justice proceeds from love, the trinitarian love of God, or are these "separate but equal" virtues in God?

---

45. See the discussion in Wolterstorff, *Justice in Love*, 71.
46. Wolterstorff, *Justice in Love*, 72.
47. Wolterstorff, *Justice in Love*, 72.

The "Double Love" of God and Neighbor

"And Who Is My Neighbor?": The Desire to "Justify" Oneself

The "lawyer's" question, "wanting to justify himself," echoes through the centuries (Luke 10:29). He has heard Jesus' answer to his question about eternal life and law, summed up in the two great commandments, to love God and to love the neighbor (Luke 10:25–28). He pretends he wants Jesus to make himself clearer (More obscure verbiage by a theologian, no doubt!). However, Luke is aware that he simply wants "to justify himself" when he asks, "And who is my neighbor?" Jesus' response is the parable of the Good Samaritan. How does this tale make a difference? Where is Christ in this parable?

Fellowship with God is often something human beings do not want. It seems "unpractical, difficult and undesirable."[48] We want to be alone, Withdrawal into ourselves can become the sin of sloth, Barth contends.[49] The neighbor becomes a burden to our freedom. Behind that is the burden of fellowship with God. Yet all people, "even the most deformed and unnatural, are elected and created and determined for fellow-humanity, for neighborly love."[50]

Jesus' response with the parable of the Good Samaritan says something about Jesus. He does not ignore the lawyer's attempt to justify himself by asking the question, "And who is my neighbor?" When Jesus becomes a friend and not just a teacher, he takes a cataclysmic step, it appears to be lowering himself (John 15:15).[51] "Neighbor" cannot be far behind.

The "who" that is my neighbor might not be just my friend, according to the lawyer. He might be only those to whom I have a commitment, such as a beloved; or even an economic or social commitment. "We can't love everyone," we can hear the lawyer say. Maybe I am just to give people their rights, the way of justice. Is that not the way of "normative social bonds?"[52]

The neighbor is not just anyone. He may have done me wrong. I may want him to repent, especially before I forgive him. Wolterstorff believes that such an action needs to be done, an "altered relation," for nowhere does Jesus tell us to forgive our enemies, only to love them.[53] This seems

---

48. Barth, *CD* IV/2, 408.
49. Barth, *CD* IV/2, 407–8.
50. Barth, *CD* IV/2, 407.
51. Barth, *The Only Way*, 92, 97.
52. Wolterstorff, *Justice in Love*, 91.
53. Wolterstorff, *Justice in Love*, 172–75.

to me to be an unwarranted separation between forgiveness and love. The answer to the question, "And who is my neighbor?" reinforces this. This may be someone I do not know, or perhaps someone I know, even that has wronged, who has not yet repented, who refuses to repent. I am still to bind up his bandages. God in Christ does not wait for us to repent before he showers grace upon us; but having done so, we then have the greatest possible motivation for repentance. The moral fact has been altered already, not by the repentance of the guilty party but by Christ's vicarious repentance. That is how deep and wide the vicarious humanity of Christ is.

The Neighbor on the Road

As we have seen, there is a vicarious action in loving the neighbor who is the person at hand, in place of and representing all of humanity. In the one "on the road" humanity is made concrete, so love should act concretely. The incarnation reminds us that God did not simply come to humble himself, but to be in solidarity with us. That is why Karl Barth and T. F. Torrance stress so strongly that the *being* of God is found in his *act*. God did not just come into humanity but became human. Torrance's concern, despite the criticisms of Douglas Farrow, is that we find no other place—in nature, Mary, the church, or sacraments—where we know God except for his specific act but in the incarnation.[54] Criticized by Farrow as possessing an "actualist ontology" and denying the humanity of Christ for a kind of Eutychianism, Torrance's center in the incarnation is rather his attempt both to allow knowledge of God to come through grace as well as take seriously our particular humanity through the particular humanity of Jesus. This is quite far from Eutychianism (overemphasizing the deity of Christ to the exclusion of the humanity). No, indeed, God has been creating a community of *reciprocity*, beginning with Israel, and fulfilled in the vicarious *response* of Christ.[55] Possessing knowledge of God in the act of Jesus Christ is genuine knowledge of God, but Torrance, along with Karl Barth, is not saying it is exhaustive knowledge of God. Yet this knowledge of God is not without humanity: As an act of God, the incarnation is still "done into our humanity, wrought out in our place and as our act."[56] To say that

---

54. Farrow, "T. F. Torrance and the Latin Heresy," *First Things*, 29–30.

55. T. F. Torrance, *God and Rationality*, 162–63 and *The Mediation of Christ*, Second Edition, 12–15.

56. T. F. Torrance, "Atonement and the Oneness of the Church," 243.

The "Double Love" of God and Neighbor

Barth does not have a revelation of God in Christ that has "duration" (Bonhoeffer in *Act and Being* and Farrow) ignores the significance of the living Lord Jesus Christ for Barth's theology, so that, for Barth, "the statement that He, Jesus Christ, lives ... is at once the simplest and the most difficult Christological statement."[57] For the neighbor, this means that we take one's particular humanity very seriously. The solidarity between God and humanity in the incarnation does mean, however, that we will be challenged by God becoming like us, an equal, if you will. What is important is that neighbor love is recognizing the other as equal.[58] This is highly problematic for many people and their doctrines of God. Is humanity equal with God? However, this is not the "condescension of preferential love," another kind of self-love. The miracle of the incarnation, and Christ's faith in the Father, is that he makes himself equal with humanity. Eschatologically, the darkness of the world that hides the victory of Christ is illumined by love for the neighbor.[59]

Faith and hope are bound up in genuine love for the beloved (1 Cor 13). How much more is this true in the love of the Father for the Son and the Son for the Father? "Love believes all things" (1 Cor 13:7), even in what is not seen, or in the one who is misguided or lost.[60] Yet how can love for the one on the road necessarily be knowledge?[61] The Samaritan did not know the man. However, what he did know of the man was that he was the neighbor; he was the one he encountered on the road; on that road, no other road, at no other time.

"Love hopes all things" (1 Cor 13:7) means that one never gives up on the one loved.[62]

"Care" speaks of the active kind of love that one exhibits to the Samaritan to the man on road; a love that can both enhance and secure a person's existence; bandages, oil and wine, bringing him to the inn, etc.[63] Care is active love. Does the Father care for the Son? Does the Son care for the

---

57. Barth, *CD*, IV/3.1, 39. Cf. Barth's commendation of Bonhoeffer's *Sanctorum Communio* as "a theological miracle" (*CD* IV/2, 641). This book is the source of Bonhoeffer's famous statement, "Christ exists as community" (*Sanctorum Communio*, 141, 189, 191, 199). Of course, Bonhoeffer wrote long before the Barth of *CD* IV/3.

58. Kierkegaard, *Works of Love*, 60.

59. T. F. Torrance, *Space, Time and Resurrection*, 139.

60. Kierkegaard, *Works of Love*, 221.

61. Kierkegaard, *Works of Love*, 228.

62. Kierkegaard, *Works of Love*, 258–59.

63. Wolterstorff, *Justice in Love*, 101.

Father? Does not the Father care for the world (the doctrine of providence!) through the Son?[64] In responding to the Father, is not the Son saying on behalf of creation "Yes!" to the Father's care, despite our disobedience and ungratefulness? Care speaks of the worth of the one cared for.[65] Is this what justice requires, as Wolterstorff believes, or a gratuitous act, as Nygren argues?[66] Certainly to do justice is an act of love because to act justly demonstrates that we give one what one deserves. The Son cares because care is love in action. He cares for all not because all deserve it but because he gives us worth. We come to deserve it because God gives us the worth. It is not just an issue of God acting "fairly." The Samaritan gave the man on the road worth by his action of love towards him.

That care must not be mistaken for taking up a popular cause or conserving a tradition, or even busying ourselves in philanthropic activity and the work of the church. Karl Barth warns us all of this can be dehumanizing unless it involves "the concrete man," the neighbor on the road, we might say, not humanity in the abstract.[67] How do we avoid this temptation? Do we ask ourselves if we are seeing the neighbor with the eyes of Jesus, eyes we would not normally possess?

A "Need" for the Neighbor?

Is love a need? We have seen that Kierkegaard does not restrict "need-love" to preferential love. We have a need to love the neighbor, he will contend, not "just to have someone to love, but he needs to love people."[68] God as "the middle term" keeps this from being pride. Since it is love of the neighbor, it is unconditionally every human being, not just the ones we like. From whence, however, does this need come? Kierkegaard is less clear here. Can need-love ever avoid being preferential love? Certainly, as Kierkegaard observes, one has a "need" to see a human being after living on an uninhabited island or after being in solitary confinement. But that is certainly not what Jesus meant by the neighbor love exhibited by the Samaritan. The need-love there existed from the part of the victim of the robbers on the road. However, did Christ "need" to love us? Did he "need"

---

64. See Kettler, *The God Who Believes*, 151–57.
65. Wolterstorff, *Justice in Love*, 101.
66. Wolterstorff, *Justice in Love*, 108.
67. Barth, *CD* IV/2, 439.
68. Kierkegaard, *Works of Love*, 67.

to love the Father? One may want to see Christ in the victim, if one thinks of the parable of the sheep and the goats, in which Christ is found in the naked, sick, or in prison, "the least of these" (Matt 25:45). Yet this is based on the free act of God in becoming incarnate in Jesus Christ, a free act of becoming like us. Can love be seen as "the deepest need" in the one who loves the neighbor, as Kierkegaard claims?[69] Once again (see chapter one), we see the problem of claiming need-love in God, especially from a trinitarian perspective. The Son does not need to love the Father in response to the Father's love, which he also does not need to do. However, he does act freely to meet our needs. God loves freely, in himself, and toward us. The vicarious love of the Son to the Father on our behalf only accentuates this. Kierkegaard's problem is related to seeing divine love as duty. A command, seen in an intra-trinitarian sense, is not necessarily a duty.

The Son does not have a need to love the Father; so one should not retreat to talk about the "right" that the Father has to be loved, as is often done in "rights" discussion today. As Wolterstorff admits, "rights" discussion can degenerate into a focus on one's own entitlement, a grasping self, an obsessive individualism, and personal autonomy.[70] However, talk of "rights" can just as easily speak of the worth of the one claiming rights.[71] Could this not also be true of the worth of the Father? Is not the Son simply honoring the Father? In fact, could we have here a better foundation for human rights than simply personal autonomy, in the communion between the Father and the Son in which we now participate through the Holy Spirit?

Does the Son have a need to love the Father? Certainly, not in a sense even if, with Wolterstorff, one believes that repentance is needed in order for there to be forgiveness (thereby confusing forgiveness with reconciliation).[72] The Father has no need to love the neighbor, even through the Son, since the Son already loves him. He certainly does not need for the world as neighbor to respond since the Son has already responded with "simple obedience" (Bonhoeffer).[73] He loves the neighbor simply by grace.

---

69. Kierkegaard, *Works of Love*, 67.
70. Wolterstorff, *Justice in Love*, 90–91.
71. Wolterstorff, *Justice in Love*, 91.
72. Wolterstorff, *Justice in Love*, 172–75.
73. Bonhoeffer, *Discipleship*, 77–83.

The Neighbor and Love for God

According to Kierkegaard, neighbor love, in contrast to preferential love, is most like God.[74] In this way, however, one can continue to love the beloved, as long as love for the neighbor is "the sanctifying element in your union's covenant with God." One can love the friend as long as love for the neighbor is "what you learn from each other in your friendship's confidential relationship with God!" In other words, God's love does not choose anyone in particular, but loves all. We have seen, however, how problematic it is to withdraw freedom ("choosing") from God. Our ignorance of God is just as great as our ignorance of love; both suffer from the risk of fear of rejection and disappointment. There is a very genuine knowledge in love, especially in the knowledge of love that the Son possesses of the Father.[75] We fear an intractable God, even if he is "forced" by necessity to love. Is God then bound to love, in fact, bound to love everyone whether he wants to or not? Yet genuine love is noted by its lack of desire to possess, in contrast to lust. Should this be any less true for God?

Paternalism is always a danger, a kind of pseudo-love that brings benevolence but not care.[76] Behind paternalism is the unspoken assumption of all utilitarianism: I know that my actions will result in the greatest good for the greatest number of people, and especially for you![77] The response of Jesus to the Father is a love that has already experienced the love that is genuine care, even in light of the cross. The vicarious response of Jesus is a judgment on our ability to make those decisions. This is humble medicine indeed, yet essential to take.

Is neighbor love most like God, in contrast to a traditional theory of vicarious punishment, as Wolterstorff suggests?[78] Did not Jesus clearly teach we are not to seek retributive punishment of the wrongdoer? So why would God seek for a vicarious punishment in the blood of Jesus? Certainly, Wolterstorff has a point if atonement is seen in terms of blood sacrifice as a "trigger" for God to forgive. Yet there are truly consequences of actions (Deut 30: 15–20) that reflect the seriousness of sin for God and his love for us. Punishment does not have to be capricious. Moreover, punishment

---

74. Kierkegaard, *Works of Love*, 62–63.
75. Kierkegaard, *Works of Love*, 228.
76. Wolterstorff, *Justice in Love*, 222–23.
77. Wolterstorff, *Justice in Love*, 227, 232.
78. Wolterstorff, *Justice in Love*, 193.

does not have to be the whole or even the center of atonement. Forgiveness can even be seen as the first stage of atonement (see Mark 2 and Jesus' pronouncement of forgiveness of sins even before Calvary). The just arrangement of punishment follows from its origins in the love of the triune God, expressed in the vicarious response of the Son to the Father's love.

We are not permitted, of course, to draw a sharp distinction between Christ and the neighbor. The parable of the sheep and the goats (Matt 25) will not permit that. As we see Christ in those who are naked and without food, so we see him in the neighbor. This is why we can "confess our sins to one another" (Jas 5:16), because Christ is in our midst.[79] This becomes a reality of the vicarious humanity of Christ in the church, as one acts on behalf of another, the priestly ministry of the church, participating in the continuing priestly ministry of Christ.[80]

The Superiority of Love for the Neighbor?

Love for neighbor is said to be superior to love for the beloved or the friend, because the beloved or the friend can change or die.[81] There is always a neighbor around to love. Is this surrendering the neighbor to need-love again? Do I really love him if I love him because he is "available"? Again, we need not surrender the humanity of Christ to recognize that the Son, in his humanity, chooses to love, trust and obey the Father for our sakes and on our behalf. He could have listened to the devil and received the world, if he would "love" the devil (Matt 4:1-11; Mark 1:12-13; Luke 4:1-13), but, no, he chooses to love the Father. In this way we may be said to be "like" Christ (remembering Bonhoeffer's caveat); like him in his free choice of love for the Father, just as the Father freely loves the Son. The Son is the one who "loved me and gave himself up for me" (Gal 2:20), to the extent of interceding for me (Heb 7:25). "Intercession," says Bonhoeffer, for the Christian now becomes the "God-given means for realizing God's purpose" where "the nature of Christian love again proves to be to work 'with,' 'for,' and ultimately 'in place of' our neighbor, thereby drawing the neighbor deeper and deeper into the church-community."[82] This is where Bonhoeffer can boldly speak of "Christ existing as church-community" without equating

---

79. Bonhoeffer, *Sanctorum Communio*, 189–90.
80. See T. F. Torrance, *Royal Priesthood*.
81. Kierkegaard, *Works of Love*, 64–65.
82. Bonhoeffer, *Sanctorum Communio*, 188–89.

the church with Christ.[83] It lives by the Word and the Spirit alone. The church is no longer seen as a means to an end, however, but as community of neighbor love, as an end in itself, yet open to the world.[84]

The question of "how" can we love our often annoying if not detestable neighbor can become a question divorced from the being of God known in his act in Jesus Christ, the Son who loves when it is difficult, if not impossible, to love the neighbor. Always helpful is C. S. Lewis's counsel concerning the difficulty of loving one's neighbor: "Do not waste time bothering whether you 'love' your neighbor; act as if you did. As soon as we do this, we find one of the great secrets. When you are behaving as if you loved someone, you will presently come to love him."[85] So also, for Dostoevsky, proof for faith is not available, but it is possible to become convinced by "the experience of active love."[86] We are saved from living a lie and hypocrisy (did not Jesus judge the heart?) by the active love of the Son for the Father in which we participate. We are not alone in our quest to be more loving. Genuine love is vicarious, Bonhoeffer claims, even taking the place of the presence of "the community with God"![87] Genuine love must even be willing to be without the community of God, submitting to the wrath of God for the sake of the wider community. This is part of the "being-with-each-other" of the church-community.[88] Bonhoeffer's own imprisonment experience may be a grim example of that. These acts of love, however, can never be found in any one person, apart from Christ, in contrast to Roman Catholic views of merit.[89] Bonhoeffer presents three possibilities of acts of love that involve a genuine intention to self-denial: "*self-renouncing, active work for the neighbor; intercessory prayer; and, finally, the mutual forgiveness of sins* in God's name."[90] All of these are part of renouncing happiness and advocating vicariously for others, to give up one's own advantage, and that may include, startlingly, "our community with God itself," a willingness to submit oneself to God's wrath for the sake of others, as Moses and Paul demonstrate (Exod 32:32; Rom 9:1ff). How can Bonhoeffer say this?

83. Bonhoeffer, *Sanctorum Communio*, 189, 191, 199.
84. Bonhoeffer, *Sanctorum Communio*, 190, 304.
85. C. S. Lewis, *Mere Christianity*, 116.
86. Dostoevsky, *The Brothers Karamazov*, 56–58.
87. Bonhoeffer, *Sanctorum Communio*, 184–85.
88. Bonhoeffer, *Sanctorum Communio*, 182.
89. Bonhoeffer, *Sanctorum Communio*, 183.
90. Bonhoeffer, *Sanctorum Communio*, 184.

The "Double Love" of God and Neighbor

Echoes must be seen here of the cry of abandonment from the cross. Jesus is separated from the Father for our sakes. Even community is not an end itself, with God or others, but love of the neighbor.

In love for the neighbor, Jesus Christ is for the neighbor. Atonement takes on the moral meaning of being for another. Usually we believe that only our friends and lovers are for us. We can count on them being for us. However, in Jesus Christ we know that God is for us, to the point of doing something on our behalf and in our place. Loving your neighbor as Christ loves your neighbor is to give new life, as Kierkegaard reminds us, not only to erotic love, but also to friendship love. Neighbor love demonstrates its superiority by transforming erotic love and friendship love.

The Claim of God

To accept the claim of God is to relativize the "transfiguration" that the poets say happens with erotic love.[91] The lover may renounce all the claims of life for the sake of the beloved, but one is not close to neighbor love until one realizes the "enormous claim" of God. Otherwise, one stays in the childish state of "me wants." One stays with paganism. "Do not the pagans also do the same?" as Jesus comments on those who "greet only your brothers and sisters" (Matt 5:47), those who do not have an inkling about self-denial.[92] Such neighbor love, however, is not just based on busyness nor inaction, but on "sheer action" because it is "the fulfilling of the Law" (Rom 13:10).[93]

This kind of "objectivity" is not a cold, distant relationship, but rather that which respects the other, does not demand for the other to be something they are not. Theologically, it is the *creatio ex nihilo*, the creation out of nothing that speaks of the distinction between God and his creature as a loud manifestation of this act of his love. This is only furthered in the vicarious humanity of Christ, as he takes on our humanity and from our side acts with an objectivity of love to counter our plight.[94]

Christ is both God making the claim on humanity as well as humanity being claimed by God. In Barth's words, he is "the concrete reality and

---

91. Kierkegaard, *Works of Love*, 89–90.
92. Kierkegaard, *Works of Love*, 53.
93. Kierkegaard, *Works of Love*, 97–98.
94. T. F. Torrance, *Theology in Reconstruction*, 236.

actuality of the promise and command of God, the fulfillment of both, very God and very man, in one person amongst us, as a fellow-man."[95]

The Objectivity of Love

Such a claim by God is not simply an act by *fiat* by and all-powerful Deity. No, the act of God in Jesus Christ penetrates so deeply into us, drawing deeply "within creaturely being," while remaining God.[96] This is "the utter objectivity of love" in the atonement, in contrast to a view of love as merely a preference or a feeling.[97] Love as objective! How audacious! Justification is not just a legal declaration, but also an exchange, sharing in Christ's righteousness, because he has first shared in our fallen humanity.[98] An objective reality is involved here. This is an objectivity, according to the nature of who God is, that is nonetheless highly personal. Its goal is to open up "earth for heaven" by involving us in the communion of one God, Father, Son, and Holy Spirit.[99] It is that love which stands against and defeats sin.[100] Torrance's words are on target:

> God does not override man but recreates, reaffirms him and stands him up before himself as his dear child, and man does not seek to use or manipulate knowledge of God for the fulfillment of his own ends in self-will and self-understanding, but loves him objectively for his own sake and is so liberated from himself *that he can love his neighbor objectively also*.[101]

But do we end up sacrificing the intimacy between the Father and the Son in the Spirit for the objectivity of the neighbor? Only if we forget that it is the intimate relation in God himself.

---

95. Barth, *CD* IV/1, 53.
96. T. F. Torrance, *Theology in Reconstruction*, 234.
97. T. F. Torrance, *Theology in Reconstruction*, 236.
98. T. F. Torrance, *Atonement*, 133–34.
99. T. F. Torrance, *Theology in Reconstruction*, 238.
100. T. F. Torrance, *Theology in Reconstruction*, 238.
101. T. F. Torrance, *Theology in Reconstruction*, 237 (italics mine).

CHAPTER FOUR

The Vicarious Love of the Son for Flames, Friends, and Families

Our confusion about love, and its relation to desire, seems to reach a fever pitch when it comes to discussing what love is between lovers, spouses, and families in our postmodern age of tolerance and autonomy. Surely this is the point where love is purely defined as desire, and any question of what love is is defined by what we desire. At this point, we are at our most sensitive: our relationships, people we care most deeply about; people who raised us. However, our relationships with them are often not pretty. In fact, they are often very complicated. Ask any pastor who counsels couples regularly. I remember vividly a pastor of a large, successful, evangelical church saying once that, looking upon his congregation on a Sunday morning, half of them desperately wanted to be in a marriage and the other half desperately wanted out!

We are talking about a variety of relationships here, but all have the commonality of intimacy, or at least potential for intimacy (parents and children). The "flame" (as in "old flame") is the "sweetheart," the boyfriend or girlfriend, the not yet married, but who is to deny help for the passions of love at this point? This can be true of the first loves of teenagers or late in life lovers who find love again. It may apply to the growing number of couples that never have been married. Sometimes thought to lack intimacy, friendship love is often ignored but it is quite possibly the prevalent and perhaps deepest of all the loves. Many friendships last where marriages often crumble. "Love and marriage, love and marriage, Go together like a horse and carriage . . ." so the old song went . . . but is marriage increasingly unworkable today? In addition, is the institution of the family changing before our eyes, beyond recognition? Where is the place of the vicarious love of the Son towards the Father for the often-embattled postmodern family?

Of course, some have suggested this is where the church is seen to be most anachronistic, stifling desires of either the autonomous individual or the newly tolerant society. The films of the nineteen fifties and before are routinely mocked for "repressive" values, particularly when it comes to sex.

Where does the love, the vicarious love, of the Son for the Father, a love on our behalf and in our place, come into these relationships?

Modern Challenges and the Vicarious Love of the Son's Judgment on the Family

Do we even know what a family is today? I am not a psychiatrist, a marriage and family therapist, or even a pastor. I am a theologian. However, I can speak of the loves of our relationships from the perspective of what we see in the vicarious love of the Son for the Father on our behalf and in our behalf, the dynamic view of the atonement often ignored in the church. However, this will involve the cross, nonetheless, so there is judgment, but perhaps a kind of judgment that we will not expect.

I remember the interview with a prospective faculty member in the marriage and family department at the university where I work when I dared to ask the question, "What is a family?" He seemed taken back. You do not ask that question in polite society. It is too awkward. Why is that? In the church, we may feel like Jesus on the cross, "My God, my God, why have you forsaken me?" (Matt 27:46). Why has God forsaken us when it comes to the challenges concerning the family today? Children are different, having been raised in a digital and social media age, often resulting of a divided home. Our parents are living much longer, and more dependent upon us as they grow older, so roles that began at our birth are ironically reversed. Contemporary views of marriage, such as same-sex marriage, challenge traditional biblical and church teaching. Marriages only seem to have a 50–50 chance of surviving anyhow. In the world of singles, not having sex before marriage seems a rarity in this culture. Promiscuity is readily found on the nearest Craigslist or Internet site. The lonely single life seems to be made a bit lonelier by anonymous faces (and bodies) throughout social media. Oh, for the world of *Leave it to Beaver*! More importantly, how relevant is what was once thought to be "the biblical ideal"?

The Vicarious Love of the Son

As Ray Anderson points out in his classic study on a theology of marriage and the family, *Something Old, Something New: Marriage and Family Ministry in a Postmodern Culture*, we need to first realize that we are children of the Age of Enlightenment, the modern age. The eighteenth century, with the advent of modern science and reason developed such benefits as modern medicine.[1] However, it also brought with it a great critique of religion and any authority outside of reason in general that challenges individual freedom, liberty, or autonomy. Nonetheless, this was also accompanied by a strong individualism and therefore isolatedness, a kind of loneliness. So even today we can easily live lonely lives before our computer screens at work and then continue a lonely life in front of the screen in the evening at home and not miss a beat. Of course, the church's response to modernity has often been presented as a protest, retreating to the basic "fundamentals" while at the same time gladly using the most modern technology available for evangelism.

My parents have been gone for over ten years now. I now know what it means to be an orphan of a kind. My only relative remains my brother in San Diego. Email and telephone can keep us in touch, but technology can only be of cold comfort at times. So the "postmodern " critics have told us that the impersonal technology of reason and science will not save us. We will increasingly seek for new communities (An explanation for even radical terrorism?). Sometimes this will be in gangs, sometimes in political movements, or on Facebook. However, will it be in religion? If we are so desperate for community, nevertheless, will we bypass the family? Is it because the postmodern family gives so little love?

The Vicarious Humanity of Christ as Judgment upon the "Ideal" Lover/Spouse/Parent/Family

I have previously written about the problem of what the psychoanalyst Karen Horney used to call the "ideal" self.[2] This is the self we create as an idol, the self we think we ought to be, yet we look in the mirror every day and that self is not there. We immediately plunge into despair and shame, slowly pulling ourselves up by our "bootstraps" in order to be the "ideal"

---

1. Anderson, *Something Old, Something New*, 3.
2. Kettler, *Breadth and Depth of the Atonement*, 114–24; Horney, *Neurosis and Mental Health*.

self again. That of course is the lie of "religion" which Jesus had to face. That is the lie of "morality." That is the opposite of grace.

Therefore, our problem is more than just with the modern or postmodern worlds. Our problem is with us in the first place. Yes, we may fall short of God's goal for sexuality. Our loves can be "disordered," in Augustine's famous words. We can become obsessed with the wrong kind of love. The problem we have with *eros*, C. S. Lewis contends, is not that we might idolize the other person, especially in marriage, but that we might idolize *eros* itself, that which is based on desire and possession, which claims immortality but in reality is the most mortal of all loves.[3]

But that did not stop the first movement of grace, God's "downward" or "humanward" movement of grace in the incarnation, the Word becoming flesh, the incarnation (John 1:14). This is, first, a movement of *solidarity*, Jesus sitting at table with even the disreputable in society (Mark 2:15; Matt 9:10; Luke 5:30). This is what I will call, "Jesus joins the family at dinner." Nothing is more perilous than joining a family at dinner! Here all the family dynamics can be seen: the ones that can be played out and the ones that are carefully hidden. Nonetheless, Jesus invites himself! Jesus joins the family at dinner. It will be quite an evening (or life!).

The "inhumanity" of the family may not exist only in overt spousal or child abuse. It may be in quieter, more desperate ways. On the other hand, it may be loud and spontaneous, despite how Anders Nygren defines *agape* as "spontaneous" love.[4] By that, Nygren certainly means a freedom of love, not coerced by merit. However, as Barth claims, "ceaseless activity" can be inhuman and cloak itself behind "pure scholarship or pure art" or family respectability. All of these can become sin as "sloth" before God.[5] The Son coming to dinner with the family will interrupt our "ceaseless activity" and a "spontaneous" love that will not take the time to sit at dinner with the family!

Jesus being at dinner first means that he does not wait for us to "get our act together" to dine, to have fellowship with him. God's grace, in other words, is lavishly poured out upon all, believer and non-believer, in Jesus Christ, the Word of God who became flesh. In contrast to the Age of Enlightenment and its obsession with certainty (Descartes), Jesus meets us as we are, as "sinners," just as God met Israel, appearing on the outside just a

---

3. C. S. Lewis, *The Four Loves*, 155–57.
4. Nygren, *Agape and Eros*, 75.
5. Barth, *CD* IV/2, 439.

The Vicarious Love of the Son

Jewish carpenter. All of this is heading toward the cross, the climax of what the early Fathers called "the wonderful (or sweet) exchange" (*The Epistle to Diognetus*, 2nd century), based on 2 Cor 8:9: "For you know the grace of our Lord Jesus Christ, that though he was rich, yet for your sake he became poor, so that by his poverty you might become rich." Listen to *The Epistle to Diognetus*: "In whom could we, lawless, and impious as we were, be made righteous except in the Son of God alone! O sweetest exchange! O unfathomable work of God!"[6] Herein is the meaning of the New Testament word *katallage*, "exchange" or "reconciliation": "All this is from God, who *reconciled* us to himself Christ, and has given us the ministry of reconciliation" (2 Cor 5:18). This is why T. F. Torrance liked to speak of a vicarious *humanity* of Christ, not just vicarious *death*. As another great Scottish theologian, John McLeod Campbell put it, this is where in the cross the heart of the Father is opened up when we see the vicarious response to the Father's love in the response of the Son, Jesus.[7] This is nothing less than the manifestation of the eternal triune life of Father, Son, and the Holy Spirit.

Such an "exchange" immediately exposes our desperate need as well as the judgement upon sin, including for those who have sinned against us. Many live quite, desperate lives, not so much of guilt over some particular dastardly deed they have performed, but *shame*, deep shame for the kind of person they are or have become. This can be nurtured insidiously for years by families, and even by churches, almost silently condemning one another with codes for not being "good enough."

But Jesus has taken that shame on the cross so that the Epistle to the Hebrews exhorts its readers to "look to Jesus, the pioneer and perfecter of faith, who for the sake of the joy that was set before him endured the cross, disregarding its *shame*, and has taken his seat at the right hand of God" (Heb 12:2). Notice that the faith of Jesus confronts shame, a vicarious faith. He is "the perfecter" as well as "the pioneer" for us. Only because of Jesus' solid identification with our humanity can he do this. Torrance used the example of teaching his daughter how to walk as an example of the vicarious humanity of Christ and our faith.[8] She feebly was gripping his strong hand, but he was really making her walk, constantly strengthening her ability to walk by herself, through his strong hand. God uses the most

---

6. Fairweather, ed., *Epistle to Diognetus*, 221.
7. Campbell, *Nature of the Atonement*, 200–12.
8. T. F. Torrance, *Preaching Christ Today*, 32.

inauspicious things. God can even use the shame of the world, Hebrews says, to bind himself to the world. That is the power of God.

This is done, not just from the standpoint of the sheer power of deity, but from the side of humanity. It can become even dicier when a human relationship involves *betrayal*, something Jesus would himself very much experience. Ray Anderson suggests that we are only betrayed by those whom we love—friends, lovers, spouses, family members—this is where it becomes the most acute.[9] Love is no insurance policy against betrayal, he adds. Could it be that a family who has never faced betrayal has never had a love worthy of being tested? This, of course, reminds us to go back to Judas, one who was knowingly chosen by Jesus although he would betray him, a betrayal that would lead to the cross. Was not this betrayal the final word?

The Son has a capacity to love if he is truly human. Of course, this raises the age-old question, "Could Jesus sin?" If he is the eternal Word of God, many would say (T. F. Torrance included) that he not able to sin (*non posse peccare*).[10] This is neither as deterministic as with Augustine ("not able not to sin," *non posse non peccare*) nor as simply libertarian ("able to sin," *posse peccare*). The vicarious humanity of Christ, I believe, moves us to believe in a Son of God who had a genuine capacity of obedience or disobedience to the Father; in this case, even a capacity for betrayal. Therefore, it might be better to speak of Jesus being able not to sin (*posse non peccare*).[11] Was Gethsemane real or not? On the other hand, was it just like a church play and Jesus was just mouthing words when he said, "Thy will be done"? This speaks of a real relationship in which Jesus could have chosen to walk away from the cross, just as he chose to do the Father's will throughout his incarnate ministry.

"It was strange," Anderson imagines Judas saying in his fictional postmortem encounter with Jesus, "He did not try to talk me out of my despair and torment; he merely touched it with his own suffering."[12] The Son's capacity to suffer only mirrors God's capacity to suffer, if we truly believe in a "crucified God." Simply touching Judas with his own suffering is a ministry of grace for Judas.

---

9. Anderson, *Self-Care*, 168ff.

10. T. F. Torrance, *Doctrine of Jesus Christ*, 125, 128.

11. See the discussion of the "posses" in T. F. Torrance, *Doctrine of Jesus Christ*, 125–30.

12. Anderson, *Judas and Jesus*, 118; *Gospel According to Judas*, 149; Kettler, *Reading Ray S. Anderson*, 84.

The Son's capacity to suffer for us, vicariously, is a mirror into the heart of God, the crucified God. That is why Paul describes the Christian life as being "crucified with Christ" in Gal 2:19–20. And the life I now live I live by *the faith of the Son of God*, who *loved* me and gave himself for me." Who am I, then? Not first of all by the blood pedigree of a wealthy, famous, "acceptable" family. No, that kind of identity has become judged, crucified with Christ. How do we believe that in this obviously unjust world? By faith. However, not by our faith first, but by "the faith of the Son of God," the same one who "loved me." He reflects what God the Father thinks about the hierarchical prejudices of the classes and consanguinity in our society. Kochs and Kennedys, beware! His blood is stronger than their bloodlines. All of this is the "downward movement" of judgment, the movement of the cross leading to the vicarious humanity of Christ.

The Meaning of the Cross and Vicarious Love

In other words, the meaning of the loved ones begins not with an ideal, but with what Ray Anderson calls "crucified humanity," humanity under the cross, humanity judged by Jesus Christ.[13] This is genuine humanity, fallen, yes, yet historical and real. Humanity under judgment, but it is the judgment of Jesus Christ, the judgment of grace. This is where theological subtlety comes into play. "Crucified humanity" is how we find human beings, but we do not find them without any idea of what it means to be human. This is not an ideal, however, but the humanity of Jesus Christ. Therefore, this is where there is a criterion for illness based on knowledge of the healthy one: the healthy one being the sinless man, Jesus Christ.[14] He tells us what it means to be perfectly faithful and obedient to the Father. He lives the life we are unable to live, so he lives it vicariously, on our behalf and in our place. Nevertheless, this is genuine knowledge of humanity. This becomes all too important in the closest of our relationships, including the family, whoever might be involved in sexual relationships that do not meet God's goal for humanity. Sometimes we know too much about them; sometimes they know too much about us. We need a *mediator;* we need Someone to come between us, to give us some air at times.

What would happen if Jesus came to dinner?

---

13. Anderson, *On Being Human*, 16ff.
14. Anderson, *On Being Human*, 17, 29.

The Descent of the Son: Jesus Comes to Dinner

We glibly speak, and sing, of "the Word becoming flesh," "incarnation," but what if he sat down with the family, with our loved one, with our spouses, with our children, what would he say? What would he do? What would he find? What would we say? What would we do?

First, we would find out how we can speak of God and humanity. Dietrich Bonhoeffer put it so frankly: "Whoever looks at Jesus Christ sees in fact God and the world at one. From then on they can no longer see God without the world, or the world without God."[15] We are now connected with one another because of the incarnation of God in Jesus Christ. So the Son's love for the Father, and the Father's love for the Son, should have something to say for our relationships, should it not? However, what it will say should not bypass the cross, the judgment upon our ideas of both God and humanity, including the family and loving relationships. This will be hard, so hard, because we have so much invested in them; witness the furor over same-sex marriage in recent years. However, Jesus is bringing us to a point of vulnerability, "crucified humanity," before there is any freedom, let alone autonomy. Here is the place of the cross. Most of all, God connects us with himself in Jesus. He takes responsibility for us in this descent, this descent of sitting at table with us, taking responsibility upon himself *vicariously*.[16] He has become the "kinsman-redeemer," the *goel* of the book of Ruth, who redeems us out of our poverty and slavery by solidarity in blood and property.[17]

"Crucified humanity" means that Jesus was not a "successful man," Bonhoeffer drolly comments.[18] No "dress for success" here! The world idolizes success. Therefore, Christ as the crucified one always in a sense is an alien to the world. The judgment of grace is a judgment "out of sheer love."[19] "Over against the successful, God sanctifies pain, lowliness, failure, poverty, loneliness, and despair in the cross of Christ. Not that all this has value in itself; it is made holy by the love of God, who takes it all and bears it as judgment."[20] There is nothing inherent in weakness or loneliness that

---

15. Bonhoeffer, *Ethics*, 82.
16. T. F. Torrance, *Incarnation*, 241.
17. T. F. Torrance, *Atonement*, 44.
18. Bonhoeffer, *Ethics*, 88–90.
19. Bonhoeffer, *Ethics*, 90.
20. Bonhoeffer, *Ethics*, 90.

The Vicarious Love of the Son

is valuable, Bonhoeffer hastens to add, but only in their acceptance by the divine love.

How hard is it to hear the words that judge the "successful" person! What parent does not want their child to be "successful"? How many would-be spouses would admit that they do not value a potential marriage partner's "success"? Does not Jesus expose all those things in our dinner conversation?

Those we are most intimate with, the flames, the friends, and the families, need to see that Christ came so intimately to us that he took up our humanity and acted upon our behalf. In doing so, he provides a forgiveness that does not bypass judgment; indeed, it implies judgement upon our sin. James B. Torrance speaks of the Scottish theologian John McLeod Campbell's view of atonement as presenting forgiveness on the cross that implies judgment.[21] That is because it was worked out in terms of Christ's vicarious humanity. His life was lived in perfect oneness with the Father, representing both the Father to humanity, and humanity before the Father.

All of this is saying that the vicarious response of love of the Son to the Father is not without the cross as a prelude, indeed, a crucial prelude of judgment. The vicarious humanity of Christ does not come without the cross and judgment. In today's culture, judgment is not a nice word.

Of course, we do need judgment for our loved ones. Judgment is another way of saying we want justice in our families. Violence is too often perpetrated from without, and sadly, from within, the family. Ray Anderson tells the story of the abused woman who never had the opportunity to see her abusive father brought to trial. Anderson set up a mock "trial," which then found the father guilty, and a great peace came over her. A judgment had been pronounced. Justice had been done.

The judgment had to be made by God. We can be unsure how a human judge or jury can make a judgment. Here is the God who is both the judge and the judged. We need this for our families because the hurts are too deep, the pains have been endured for too long of a time. Jesus was not just a man sent from God but "God was in Christ reconciling the world to himself" (2 Cor 5:19). This same God was on the cross. "We needed an incarnate God, a God put to death," said Gregory Nazianzen, "that we might live. We were put to death together with him, that we might be cleansed; we rose again with him..."[22]

---

21. J. B. Torrance, "New Introduction," 13.
22. Gregory Nazianzen, *Or.*, 45.28f, cited by T. F. Torrance, *The Trinitarian Faith*.

Yet judgment is not enough. New life is needed. Resurrection of new life is needed. This is where the vicarious humanity, not just death, of Christ comes to help our flames, our friends, and our families, all of those who are most dear and intimate to us, to those who know us best. For we cannot view Christ any longer at a distance. We may want to, but we can no longer do so. Bonhoeffer speaks again: "What happened to Christ has happened for all, for he was *the* human being."[23]

The Ascent of the Son: The Family Leaves with Jesus

The resurrection of Jesus culminates with his ascent, his ascent to the right hand of God (Phil 2:9), the climax of the "Godward" movement of the incarnation. This movement is part of Christ's humanity, his vicarious humanity, for us and in our place.

The resurrection, of course, includes his exaltation. It is in God's freedom that we participate in Christ's exaltation (Phil 2:5–11).[24] As Barth puts it, in a play on a saying of the Fathers, "God became man in order that man may—not become God, but come to God."[25] The ontological distinction between God and the creature is still there, but there is genuine exaltation of humanity in the exaltation of the Son. Our humanity does not stop with being forgiven of our sins, as important as that is. Justification demands sanctification, demands holiness, or wholeness, but not a sanctification that depends upon us.[26] Christ is the one who is sanctified, the one who is exalted. We participate in his exaltation and sanctification. Therefore, the development of the incarnation in the atonement means the revelation of sanctification that has already taken place.[27] This is no "ideal" humanity, but who we are now, though we do not "appear" to be (1 John 3:2). Our heavenly destiny is not to be slighted (as N. T. Wright repeatedly does),[28] but is to be seen in light the exaltation of the vicarious humanity of Christ, which involves the entirety of our humanity, including the entirety of our relationships, especially those of intimacy. The "higher level" of exaltation

---

142.

23. Bonhoeffer, *Ethics*, 91.
24. Barth, *CD* III/4, 524.
25. Barth, *CD* IV/2, 106.
26. Barth, *CD* IV/2, 517.
27. T. F. Torrance, *Incarnation*, 66; Campbell, *Nature of the Atonement*, 20.
28. Wright, *The Day the Revolution Began*, 223.

The Vicarious Love of the Son

is not "an abstractly spiritual life, of pure inwardness." This is "a matter of man's life in its totality, of man as the soul of his body, and therefore of the outward life . . ."[29] These words of Karl Barth's apply no less to our "flames, friends, and families"—those whom we hold most dear—but are most problematic for us! Again, the "ideal" is to be rejected in favor of what Barth calls "earthiness."[30]

As there is the *kenosis*, of "emptying" of God in becoming human (Phil 2:5–11), a descent that follows with an ascent, so that act of becoming a servant has a correspondence in our self-denial of ourselves.[31] However, one should be careful to see that this self-denial is not outside of the vicarious humanity of Christ, not outside Christ's faith and repentance that upholds us. Then we can participate in his resurrection, ascension, and exaltation. Otherwise, self-denial becomes just another religious act.

The platonic tradition of spirituality depends heavily on the "ascent" of the soul up "Jacob's ladder" or the "mountain," a process of *purification, illumination, and union.*[32] However, where are our relationships of intimacy—flames, friends, and families—in this? Are they left behind for us to take this individualistic spiritual journey alone? Moreover, do we end up leaving the vicarious humanity of Christ alone as well?

Certainly, *eros* and its sensibility begins this journey up the mountain, but with the goal of leaving sensible things, the things of the senses, behind.[33] This is *eros's* famous love for the beautiful and the good.[34] Note that this is not the Divine stooping down to humanity, but *eros* being the means to reach the Divine.[35] The contradiction with grace could not be greater, it seems to me. The goal is, first, "purification" of desire, not to be dead to sin (Eph 2:5).[36]

This exalted Christ, the ascended Jesus, applies no less to those lonely without or within families. The family can be a refuge for those who feel shut out by the world. The exalted Christ is their refuge, for he takes with him their humanity. My mother tells me that as a young child, she asked me

---

29. Barth, *CD* IV/2, 316.
30. Barth, *CD* IV/2, 318.
31. T. F. Torrance, *Incarnation*, 77–78.
32. Nygren, *Agape and Eros*, 572.
33. Nygren, *Agape and Eros*, 170.
34. Nygren, *Agape and Eros*, 175.
35. Nygren, *Agape and Eros*, 178, 210.
36. Nygren, *Agape and Eros*, 439.

who my friends were, and my only response was, "my comic books." Like many, I meant it. For every athlete, cheerleader, or musician the schools eagerly support, there are thousands of kids that never fit in. The love of the crucified One who was ascended is not based on one's athletic or musical skills. We all want that affirmation from others, but I can't help but remember when, years ago, my pastor Bob Myers told me of a study that said of all the professions the pastor was the one that needed the most affirmation, yet of all of them, received the least! "I need all the friends I can get! said Charlie Brown once. In addition, we then become adults and realize, not only is there a scarcity of friends; there are those who do not like you in the first place. "What a friend we have in Jesus" takes on new meaning.

However, there is Someone waiting for us, to take us with him, with whom we are already, mysteriously with, in heaven. It is this ascended Jesus who was both elected and rejected for us, Karl Barth constantly reminds us. "He elected our rejection."[37] We do not have to bear the burden of rejection.

The contemporary family, friends, and flames are confronted with a plethora of models of reality to choose from in our pluralistic society. Ray Anderson suggests that many can be boiled down to three: 1) the metaphysical, 2) the existential, and 3) the behavioral.[38] The metaphysical might believe in deeper ingrained laws of order, moral as well as physical, that direct the universe. Right and wrong can be easily discerned. The existential argues for the reality of the authentic self, the self that refused to be conformed to society. This self seeks to find itself in a society that constantly seeks to suppress it. The behavioral view values that which would be effective for the family, for example, to function well in society. This would be known by social scientific experimentation.

One can argue for each of these to possess "Christian" attributes in a sense, but Anderson contends that Christ is not bound to any of these models. Is Jesus just after "order," or being "authentic," or what is just "effective" in our lives, especially in the lives of our most intimate and valued relationships? For example, "order" in a biblical and theological sense is different than the often mechanistic, cause-and-effect sense we have of order. This often can lead to legalistic, inhumane relationships—flames, friends, or families. T. F. Torrance argues for a "contingent" order that is common to both good theology and good science.[39] We must presuppose order for any

---

37. Barth, *CD* II/2, 164.
38. Anderson, *Something Old, Something New*, 15.
39. For what follows see T. F. Torrance, "The Concept of Order in Theology and

The Vicarious Love of the Son

endeavor in human society. However, where is the origin of order? Order in theology is found in God as love, for this is who God is in himself. This does not entail a necessary connection of the world to God, as in pantheism or panentheism, but sees the world as the result of the "overwhelming, overflowing love that he freely and ungrudgingly brought the world into being, giving it a genuine reality of its own though utterly differentiated from himself."[40] Despite the way this order has been clouded by sin and evil, the Son's response to the Father is lived on our behalf and in our place, a virtual overflowing of love that we cannot perform. Perhaps this is true when we are unable to love, or even express love, to our flames, friends, or families, or when we feel unloved. This is when we should look to the Son, who, through the Spirit, can enable us to participate in his overflowing of love for them in particular, despite what we might know about them so intimately, and what they might know about us.

The new order in Jesus is not any interruption of that which is natural, but, rather, Torrance contends, that which is truly natural, the "new creation" of Christ (2 Cor 5:17).[41] Even the natural scientist is not to view the world in terms of a mechanistic (metaphysical) or behaviorist way, rather in terms of "intrinsic ontological grounds," Torrance contends.[42] The existential may simply be a reflection of personal autonomy, and nothing more. This may say much to a society that needs to see what Torrance calls a *contingent* order of the universe to God.[43] By "contingent," he means a genuine dependence on God, yet with a genuine independence still granted.

Such a view of God and the world means that there is order beyond the "authentic" self. Intimacy is not simply defined by what feels right. This has much to say concerning the definition of marriage. Is there not an order based on male and female differentiation as the Christian tradition has always claimed, contra same-sex marriage or transgender identity? The love of the Son, responding to the Father in the Spirit, is based on the command of God, an order that is not mechanistic but it is nonetheless a relational, yet ontological order, reflecting the ontological Trinity. It is also a judgment upon cruelty and just rudeness among flames, boyfriends and girlfriends, simply because one can be cruel and rude through the power of sexual

---

Science," *The Christian Frame of Mind*, 17–34.

40. T. F. Torrance, *The Christian Frame of Mind*, 19.
41. T. F. Torrance, *The Christian Frame of Mind*, 19–21.
42. T. F. Torrance, *The Christian Frame of Mind*, 26.
43. T. F. Torrance, *The Christian Frame of Mind*, 20.

manipulation. It is a judgment upon our ideas of sexual intimacy, whether or not we value commitment as intertwined with intimacy. It is a judgment even upon how we treat friends. "I have called you friends," said Jesus in the Fourth Gospel (John 15:15). Do we take that seriously enough?

What is the Jesus the Son doing now? Of course, this is the doctrine of the ascension. As Peter said in his sermon on the Day of Pentecost: "This Jesus God raised up, and of that all of us are witnesses. Being therefore *exalted* at the right hand of God, and have received from the Father the promise of the Holy Spirit, he poured out this that you both see and hear" (Acts 2:32–33). Christ has ascended, being the agent of the giving of the Holy Spirit and the church, where as our High Priest, he intercedes for us forever, the Epistle to the Hebrews tells us (Heb 7:24–25).

The church, a new "family of faith" has been created, (Gal 6:10) that will have major implications for how we view natural, human families. The family will "ascend" with Jesus and be re-created, although this is often resisted in some churches that either, on the one hand, are desperate to preserve what they call "family values" that are more traditional than biblical, or, on the other hand, those who simply recreate "families" into whatever they or the culture may desire. However, the church of Jesus Christ, participating in the vicarious humanity of Christ, will be enabled to be a "vicarious family" for those whose own families have been shattered by divorce, abuse, or violence.

The church as a "vicarious family" has to see a place, first of all, in parenting. Parenting is of foremost concern theologically and personally, before marriage. We are all products of parenting, good or bad, or the lack of it. Parents became our first theological teachers. Even Thomas Torrance, who studied with Karl Barth, said that his finest theological teacher was his mother! From our parents, as one very important example, either we learn the unconditional freeness of grace and love, or we learn that to be loved is always based on meeting certain conditions.

Parenting is essential to that process of moving from being a human to becoming a person. Here we will see that there may very well be an ontological preference based on the Word of God in Scripture for being parented by a mother and a father, a male and a female. Ray Anderson would say this is God's "preference" (perhaps not the strongest words. Would "command" be too strong?). Re-naming marriage or parenting should not be on the agenda of the church.[44] "Preference" or even "Command" can always be

---

44. Anderson, "Homosexuality: Theological and Pastoral Considerations," 280–81;

subjected to "Presence" (see Mark 2:23–28!). The presence of God is still there in a less than perfect, "tragic" situation. That is where the vicarious humanity of Christ holds us up.

The person we are to become, in being "conformed to the image of his Son" (Rom 8:29), is profoundly *social*. The distinction of being male or female is a main indicator of that. The triune nature of God teaches us that. So does the church as the family of God. The foundation goes back to that triune God, and the Son's economic manifestation in the vicarious humanity of Christ, the manifestation of his relationship with the Father. The relationship can take us back to our humanity in the garden: It was not good for Adam to be alone (Gen 2:18).

What do we find, however, in the economic relationship between the Father and the Son? We find the fatherhood of God, something that has been misused so often so we no longer speak of it easily. Is this the God of wrath? The male God? However, what if he is the God known only through the Son (Matt 11:27; Luke 10:22)? We do know that he comes as a judge upon our reflex ideas of "self-development." The Son who does the will of the Father (Matt 6:10), "learns obedience" (Heb 5:8). However, he is not a contemporary indulgent parent. Nonetheless, he is "Abba," that Aramaic term of endearment and intimacy, but not to the exclusion of transcendence (Mark 14:36; Rom 8:15; Gal 4:6).[45] Through the Father and the Son we achieve the true meaning of personhood: sons and daughters of God (Gal 4:5).

We have suggested that the family will meet up now with another family, the church. What will this mean? Will there be a rivalry? Will one have to choose one or the other? It certainly may seem so, particularly if we go back to some things Jesus said about the family. With his family asking for him, Jesus replied, "'Who are my mother and brothers?' And looking at those who sat around, he said, 'Here are my mother and my brothers! Whoever does the will of God is my brother and sister and mother!'" (Mark 4:31–35). Matthew and Luke are even stronger on the cost of discipleship, speaking of a division within families because of allegiance to him, "a man against his father," etc. "One's foes will be members of one's own household." This is what it means to "take up the cross and follow me" (Matt 10:34–39). In Luke, the hyperbole is even to the point of "hate mother and father" to be Jesus' disciple (Luke 14:26–27). "Family values," indeed!

Something Old, Something New, 143.

45. Smail, *The Forgotten Father*, 39.

All of this hyperbole constantly goes back to the cross and the exhortation to "take up the cross." Is this a separate cross from that of Jesus? Or is this the cross of the vicarious humanity of Christ, with whom we have been crucified (Gal 2:20)? Allegiance to the kingdom is put here in terms of hyperbole, but hyperbole that is indeed meaningful. The church is there as "the family of faith," as a support for families, to direct them to the love the Son has for the Father.

But this can also be a judgment on the idol worship of the family in the church, in case that occurs. The family is not God. We have all been "crucified with Christ," including our ideas of the "ideal" family. To paraphrase Gal 2:20 to emphasize the family's participation in the vicarious humanity of Christ: The family has been "crucified with Christ, and it is no longer *the family* who lives, but it is Christ who lives in *the family*. And the life *the family* who now lives in the flesh lives by the faith of the Son of God who loved *the family* and gave himself for *the family*."

CHAPTER FIVE

Is Love Essential to Our Humanity?

What does it mean to be human? is not a self-evident question. Are we more or less than other animals? Is it the brain that makes us distinctive? Or the will? Or can it be love? How can that be if other animals share that "mother-love" instinct? Do we really need love or to be "in love" in order to have a fulfilled life? Are ascetics and celibates happier, or at least godlier? The distinctive theological question we are asking is, *How does the love with which the Son responds to the Father make our humanity different?*

"We Are Far Too Easily Pleased" (C. S. Lewis)[1]

Kierkegaard, in one of his sarcastic moods, imagines that for many the basic human values are "to be well off and yet easily manage to become someone."[2] How much human endeavor is devoted to "become someone"? Why do many view the Academy Awards as the pinnacle of human success? Winning the Oscar may mean you are simply popular, never an aspiration of Kierkegaard (or Jesus). If this is our goal, his advice is to "forget God." For it is he who created us out of nothing, to whom we "unconditionally owe everything."

---

1. C. S. Lewis, *The Weight of Glory*, 2.
2. Kierkegaard, *Works of Love*, 102.

The Original Human?

Traditionally, since Augustine, Christian theology has believed that the first state of humanity existed in original innocence, walking with God in the garden of Genesis. According to Augustine, this "enjoyment of God" existed without any want, disease, decay, and with perfect health.[3] Since modern evolutionary thought this has been seriously challenged, with resultant theological anthropologies advocating an originally "immature" Adam who will evolve into Christlikeness.[4] However, even if such an original state existed, these are not the human beings like us, who "forget God," as we devote our lives to "becoming someone." We may seek to be this "ideal" self, yet end up living a dualistic existence, our minds separated from our histories. This cannot help but affect how we view love—of God or erotic and friendship love, which certainly more than any other virtue or emotion is liable to die the death of thousand fantasies. This is in opposition to our source, and the source of love, the God to whom we "unconditionally owe everything," in Kierkegaard's words.

We seek to be someone else. Yet Jesus seeks to be a human, a human for the sake of other humans, a vicarious human. He only does this as the man who is a man for God.[5] He is the true man, the man of the covenant, who responds, as Israel was to have responded to Yahweh: "I will be your God and you will be my people."[6] This is a prohibition against seeing humanity in any other way. Jesus, even in humanity's own power or freedom of choice defines what it means to be human, not in the whimpering narcissism of our individual, myopic petty obsession over ourselves, but as the "cosmic being" who nonetheless is the man for others. Jesus defines humanity, indeed, as fellow-humanity, not for a cause or for "progress." The burden of Jesus is "easy" and "light" Karl Barth contends because *the demand is to be who we are.*[7] However, this demand does not come from within our hearts, but from outside. It is the Word of God, "which is inserted into our heart by him," the Word which "is Christ Himself." On the other hand, he "takes the place of God," in Barth's startling words (the vicarious *deity* of Christ, we might put it), because of the great need of humanity. *Cur Deus*

---

3. Augustine, *City of God*, Bk. 14, Ch. 26; 590.

4. Hick, *Evil and the God of Love*, 203; Pannenberg, *Anthropology in Theological Perspective*, 57.

5. Barth, *CD* III/2, 208.

6. Barth, *CD* IV/1, 43.

7. Barth, *CD* I/2, 386.

Homo? Why did God become human? Nicaea had this answered centuries before Anselm: "for us and our salvation."

God Becomes Human

Into this pathos comes the incarnation of God in Jesus Christ, God entering into creation and particularly as a human being. At least what must be said about this is its testament to the uniqueness of humanity, in fact, an affirmation of a special place in creation as the *priest to creation*, a common theme in the Fathers and T. F. Torrance.[8] According to Torrance, God uses this "redemptive mission" of humanity, including both theological and natural science, to heal and redeem the current twisted order, but only as humanity itself is being healed at a deep, ontological level.[9] This is the love of God at work, but not apart from humanity. "Love abides" according to the apostle (1 Cor 13:13) and Kierkegaard, because there is a third behind the two lovers who love, God, as much as he was with the incarnate Christ.[10] The one who "abides" in love acquires love at every moment, Kierkegaard claims, regardless of the situation. One might see a reflection here of his teaching on being "contemporary" with Christ.[11] We might add that the vicarious humanity of Christ continues as the one in his exalted humanity who continues to minister through the pouring out of his Spirit upon us (Acts 2:33). The benefits of the incarnation continue in the abiding of the love of God with us in a broken world and our broken lives.

A sacrifice is made because Jesus Christ reveals that to be human is to offer yourself to God; not that to be human is to appease God, as one might think; the closeness of the Father and Son relationship will not allow that. Sacrifice is a manifestation of love.[12]

God is not afraid to go into our death. He is not afraid of our humanness, including our death.[13] We often have a notion of God in which there is no place for such a humiliated God in the midst of such ordinary or "messy" lives as ours, let alone into the abyss that is death. The cry of abandonment, "My God, my God, why have you abandoned me?" brings

---

8. T. F. Torrance, *The Ground and Grammar of Theology*, 1–14.
9. T. F. Torrance, *Divine and Contingent Order*, 138.
10. Kierkegaard, *Works of Love*, 300–301.
11. Kierkegaard, *Practice in Christianity*, 36–53.
12. Schmemann, *For the Life of the World*, 35.
13. Alan E. Lewis, *Between Cross and Resurrection*, 92.

its obvious problem. Has God left Jesus? On the one hand, is it that in the mystery of the divine-human natures not even for a moment has God left him?[14] Are we afraid to deal, however, with a God-forsaken Jesus? The dead and buried Jesus reflects that. Here is the significance of our neglect of Holy Saturday, as Alan Lewis and Hans Urs von Balthasar so eloquently remind us; the dead Jesus, yes, but also the buried Jesus of the second day, the day we often skip over in haste for Easter. We do not know what to do, Lewis reminds us, with "the buried man from Nazareth." This simply means we do not know what to do with the ragged edges and unfinished business, the unfulfilled promises and loss and lack of love in our lives, lives that lead all too quickly to the coldness of the grave. However, God does. He goes there. In the freedom of God he goes not in "cringing servility," "suppressed ill-will," or "potential revolt," but in "the choice of His grace," to be "lowly as He is exalted and exalted as He is lowly."[15] Only in this way is he crowned "the royal man."

It is in this place of death, Alan Lewis reminds us, where God should not be, that we find God, the God revealed in the crucified and buried, yes, God-forsaken Jesus, only the God who is revealed as "a servant Lord, a guilty Judge, a wounded Healer."[16]

We then know that love is essential to who God, our creator is. Then we can see how essential love is to being human. Love is not one of many attributes of God, as so much of classical theology has said. Love is the event when one can identify with another at one's lowest point, even to the point of giving one to death.[17] This life of God reveals what it truly means to be human: to live a life of sacrificial love, a life so foreign to the lives most people live.[18] We offer ourselves to God because Christ has already offered himself, Schmemann continues. That is the meaning of the Eucharist. We have nothing to offer: "Eucharist is the only full and real response of man to God's creation, redemption and gift of heaven. However, this perfect man who stands before God is *Christ*. . . . In Him alone all that God has given man was fulfilled and brought back to heaven. He alone is the perfect

---

14. Alfeyev, *Mystery of Faith*, 90.
15. Barth, *CD* IV/2, 352.
16. Alan E. Lewis, *Between Cross and Resurrection*, 91–92.
17. Alan E. Lewis, *Between Cross and Resurrection*, 99.
18. Schmemann, *For the Life of the World*, 35.

Eucharistic Being."[19] These are Schmemann's words for the vicarious humanity of Christ.

Humanity as Creatureliness

In this crucified, buried, and God-forsaken Jesus is also revealed our humanity as never before.[20] Our humanity as created by God involves creatureliness. Yet this creatureliness does not exhaust our humanity. Ray Anderson's insight is important: "Creatureliness is an undifferentiated field upon which the occasion of the human occurs."[21] What we share with other creatures is the setting, the occasion for the human, but this does not define all that a human is. It might include all of our actions such as eating, drinking, or even being religious, which can be done either as human or inhuman activities, as Barth observes.[22] Becoming human only happens in the encounter and intimacy of the I-Thou relationship that becomes "I am as Thou art." Love becomes essential, it follows, to being human, but only the kind of love that addresses a solidarity between humans, and originally with God, the author of our existence. Therefore, motherhood and work, Barth wryly comments, are not innately human! Parents and the workplace can become demonic. They can be either human or inhuman.

Yet one feature of humanity as creaturely absolutely corresponds to the Son's love for the Father: As the creature is distinct from the Creator, so the Son can be a recipient of the Word of God. One who is distinctive from the Father can be a hearer of the Word, a hearer for us who have become dull and hard of hearing.[23]

Substitutionary Atonement and Humanity

Substitutionary atonement, if it describes the vicarious humanity, not just death, of Christ, reveals an incomparable value of humanity, and of the human to the human and the human to God. If *at every point*, God takes our place in Christ, not just paying the penalty for sin, then *at every point*

---

19. Schmemann, *For the Life of the World*, 37.
20. Alan E. Lewis, *Between Cross and Resurrection*, 92.
21. Anderson, *On Being Human*, 21.
22. Barth, *CD* III/2, 249.
23. Barth, *CD* III/4, 327.

human beings are valuable to God. Possibly the most pointed question the Christian apologist might ask to "the new atheism" of today typified by Richard Dawkins, Sam Harris, Christopher Hitchens, or Daniel Dennett is: Why do you value human beings? Why am I of more value than the insects that scamper out of my garage with the light of each morning, some escaping, some to ignominiously end their already brief lives smashed by my shoe? Or why do you value human beings only for their achievements (and why is one "achievement" valued over another?), or for what one individual can get out of another?[24] For Barth, the value of the human life and the redemption of that human life is what it means for God to be a friend to humanity. Here, friendship is not a secondary kind of love, but maybe the highest. That "abiding" (John 15:4) love of the "friend" we have in Jesus (John 15:15) is the love of the friend who voluntarily values us. Like any friend, one is under no compulsion to befriend us; one simply wants to. One wants to take our place, to do and be what we are unable to do and be, even when it pertains to love.

This is no ordinary friend, however. As much as the Son is in solidarity and identification with our humanity, he is also the "man for God" who is the "man for man," indeed, a "cosmic being" a being that is a human being for others.[25] Surprisingly, it is not as God that he is the "cosmic being," but as a human being, in his vicarious humanity, the man for others, in Bonhoeffer's language. Barth hastens to add that this does not mean, however, that he is the man as an advocate of a cause, a culture, "the progressive triumph of spirit over nature," or even the "higher development" of humanity.[26] These are all too real temptations for those who seek to "serve" humanity. The *Twilight Zone* story reminds us that aliens may come declaring cheerfully their intention only to "serve" humanity.[27] What they mean, using the ambiguity of the translation into English, is to have these human dainties for dinner! "Serving" others, Barth often warns us, can mask the tyranny of an ideology that is really the master and not a love for the real person. So also, in our day, "culture" and "diversity" can easily become abstract principles that simply become new ideologies rather than serving actual human beings. No, Christ is the "cosmic man" who in his humanity

---

24. Barth, *CD* IV/3.2, 799–800.

25. Barth, *CD* III/2, 208.

26. Barth, *CD* III/2, 208.

27. "To Serve Man," *The Twilight Zone*, March 2, 1962. Written by Rod Serling, based on a story by Damon Knight. See also C. S. Lewis, *The Silver Chair*.

"takes the place of God," what we have called elsewhere "the vicarious deity of Christ," to actually help humanity in reality—not simply symbolically—to ease a guilty conscience. Pentecost is that act of universalizing the atoning vicarious humanity of Christ, creating the church, a communion of the Holy Spirit, of "those who accept the decision God has already made on their behalf in Christ's atoning life and death."[28]

The reconciliation in Christ, particularly in his act of vicarious humanity on our behalf, cannot be undone, any more than God becoming undone in the man Jesus of Nazareth can be undone.[29] Both "objective" and "subjective" response have already occurred, where "true being and true knowing are wedded together."[30] The "subjective," which we today would tend to view in the culture or in ethnic or racial diversity, is first seen in the vicarious humanity of Christ, his perfect and faithful obedience to the Father. This becomes the criterion for judgment and embracing of our cultures.[31]

Love and Creation by God

Love, in other words, is intimately connected with who we are as created by God, owing existence to God alone. "To be well off and yet easily manage to become someone" are unrealities because if you trust in them, "you lose unconditionally everything."[32] The world "cannot take everything, simply because it cannot give everything."[33] The well-known exclamation of "vanity" by Ecclesiastes can be particularly observed in romantic relationships of love. Despair comes in the feeling of emptiness, of promises dashed, expectations unfulfilled. Ecclesiastes "sees the emptiness in homes filled with furniture. He sees the futility in overly busy lives. He sees the lack of love between family members..."[34] Love makes one vulnerable. If one does not hurt when one has been rejected this means that one has not loved. "Love hurts" laments the classic Everly Brothers song so plainly. That this love can be the source of great joy at one moment and great despair at the next is

---

28. T. F. Torrance, *Atonement*, 190.
29. T. F. Torrance, *Atonement*, 167.
30. T. F. Torrance, *Atonement*, 166.
31. See Kettler, *The Breadth and Depth of the Atonement*, 24–34.
32. Kierkegaard, *Works of Love*, 102.
33. Kierkegaard, *Works of Love*, 103.
34. Anderson, *Exploration into God*, 29.

characteristic particularly of *eros,* Barth observes. This undulation, rising and falling of "possession and loss, intoxication and soberness, enthusiasm and disillusionment, is a tragic and therefore a melancholy business."[35] Yet Ecclesiastes gains a wisdom: He now knows the limits of being human, and perhaps of the limits of our ability to love. The Sabbath rest tells us something about our limits: we need rest as well, when we trust in God's providence.[36] Is Ecclesiastes preparing us for the vicarious love of Christ? Herein is both judgment and grace. God can take everything away, only "to give everything."[37] Rejecting grace is sin, as Barth remarks: "The doctrine of the autonomy of the free creature over against God is simply the theological form of human enmity against God's grace."[38] What is this, Barth contends, but a lack of love for grace? Despondency ignores that "love abides" in what God gives and is continuing to give.[39] This is the same One who as the Son continues to love the Father for us.

Creation itself is an act of grace. That we are created as finite and limited means that, as Barth suggests, the lover has found his object of love and is "satisfied."[40] Here is another significance of the rest of God on the seventh day. That rest speaks of God's satisfaction with the "very good" of creation, especially with humanity made in his image (Gen 1:26–27). He no longer desires another kind of creation, an "emerging" monist or pantheistic entity, but is satisfied with the goodness of his finite and limited creation. Because of the existence of the Triune God in relationship, there is no need for God to create an "otherness."[41]

This is the satisfaction of the Father in the perfect faith, obedience, worship, and service of the Son to the Father on behalf of the world. Satisfaction is not the fulfillment of a legal requirement. Rather, it is the Father's satisfaction with the actions of the Son on our behalf, what the Son has been and done for us, expressed by raising him from the dead.[42] Jesus is the "beloved Son in whom I am well pleased" (Matt 3:17; Mark 1:11; Luke 3:22). Unlike Anselm's doctrine of atonement as "satisfying" the wounded

---

35. Barth, *CD* IV/2, 788.
36. Barth, *CD* III/4, 639.
37. Kierkegaard, *Works of Love,* 103.
38. Barth, *CD* II/1, 586.
39. Kierkegaard, *Works of Love,* 300–301.
40. Barth, *CD* III/1, 215.
41. Barth, *CD* II/1, 317.
42. T. F. Torrance, *Atonement,* 215.

honor of the Father by the sacrifice of the Son, this satisfaction is that of the lover who needs no other supplement to this love. He loves this one for who this one is; she does not need to be anything else. He is not the "unsatisfied" husband who philanders and prowls the streets in search of another love. Therefore, in terms of creation, God can rest on the seventh day because he is satisfied. He can also rest because he loves creation, especially humanity. The loving response of the Son is the response for us all to the wonder of this "satisfied" love, a love that knits together instead of separating creation and redemption.

The Father's satisfaction for the Son is found not in the wonders of the Son's religiosity but in the faithful and obedient Son who has united himself with humanity in its death, even as a stumbling block to all humanity, both Jews and gentiles, a crucified Messiah (1 Cor 1:23). Christ's whole ministry, Alan Lewis contends, was an extended baptism, an extended and intensive identification with humanity even at the root of its wickedness and weakness, without sinning himself.[43] At one point Jesus cries out, "I have a baptism to be baptized with; and how I am constrained until it is accomplished" (Luke 12:50). Yet he is very aware that his followers are not able to walk in his path: "Are you able to be baptized with the baptism with which I am baptized?" (Mark 10:38). No, Jesus' baptism of his entire life must be a vicarious baptism. Why is it, Alan Lewis asks in a bemusing way, that Christians grant atheists their question when they complain about a crucified God, when Christians too shrink from the eternal, immutable, impassible God becoming incarnate in this Son, yet becoming godforsaken for humanity? Why must there be limits to how closely God identifies with our hells?[44] Could it be that we still have stashed away in our homes our own "household idols," philosophical or pagan ideas of God, a God who in his majesty would never become flesh, because it would be beneath his honor and glory? The cross of the second, last Adam is a cross connected with creation, not despising it.[45]

Humans as Sinners / Human Love as Tragic

The vicarious love of Jesus, however, does not stand apart from who we are as humanity right now, as sinners. He takes on our fallen human nature in

---

43. Alan E. Lewis, *Between Cross and Resurrection*, 447.
44. Alan E. Lewis, *Between Cross and Resurrection*, 91.
45. T. F. Torrance, *Atonement*, 130.

order to heal the real person, but he does not sin in that nature himself. We do not have a high priest, Hebrews teaches us, who is unable to sympathize with our weaknesses, "but we have one who in every respect has been tested as we are yet without sin" (Heb 4:15). You cannot love me without accepting who I am now, a sinner, and in my sin. That is why to say, "I love the sinner but not the sin" is so superficial, and worse, demeaning.[46] Are you just committed to me in order to "clean me up" or do you love in the way that you will share my grief and pain, even as God seeks to transform me into the image of his Son (Rom 8:29)?[47]

The God revealed in the crucified and buried Jesus is "presence-amid-absence" in Alan Lewis's words, not afraid to live with the taunting of unbelief that challenges whether there is really a God, any true power, any true life.[48] Yet this is where we have come from, so this is where God has journeyed. The Christian message is that God cannot truly give hope, cannot truly bring healing or transformation, without this identity, this revelation of the frailty of our humanness, as much as we do not want to see it or admit it.[49] In effect, if we do not admit this finitude, we admit God has no place in our lives. It can become an excuse for atheism and unbelief. The crucified God will not allow that. A love from the side of humanity that is nevertheless divine love does not allow that, the vicarious love of Christ.

The betrayal that happened, the bad life choice that was made; the cruel words that were spoken can never be taken back. There is a "once-for-allness" of life that can never seem to be erased. Love seems hopeless. This is the reality of our finitude and our creatureliness. It takes a wicked turn when it dominates all that we are, when we end up living what T. F. Torrance calls the "nomistic" form of existence, a tragic form of existence.[50] This is when we are determined by our breaking of the law of God (*nomos*) and our guilty deeds and life determine a force of necessity in our existence. That which has been done cannot be undone. Still, Christ has come to free us from "the curse of the law" through his free grace in Jesus Christ.

"Presence-amid-absence" sounds at first nonsensical but it really demonstrates the deepest kind of inner logic of faith, the logic of love. We rarely want to equate love with the tragic, but as Ray Anderson reminds us, and

---

46. Anderson, *Self-Care*, 218–19.
47. Anderson, *Self-Care*, 218.
48. Alan E. Lewis, *Between Cross and Resurrection*, 91.
49. Alan E. Lewis, *Between Cross and Resurrection*, 92.
50. T. F. Torrance, *Space, Time and Resurrection*, 96.

Is Love Essential to Our Humanity?

the incarnate love of the Son towards the Father poured out for us shows us as well, love can very often be the stuff of the tragic. Such is the stuff of the history of the theater, of course. There is nothing inherently tragic eternally in the relationship between the Father and the Son in the Spirit. Yet the Son takes the risk of becoming human, to become a "presence-amid-absence," if you will, because love does not fear risk. Human love knows this at times when it dares to love and risks the inevitable separation by distance or death.[51] "My God, my God, why have you forsaken me?" was not playacting, but for our sake and the sake of our tragic loves throughout the centuries, chronicled by scores of tales, Shakespearean plays and heartbreaking blues music. Jesus sings the blues . . . for us.

The Life of Jesus as Atoning

The meaning of humanity is not restricted to knowing its origin and goal, even in God. Jesus' origin and goal is in God, yet the vicarious humanity of Christ teaches us that the totality of his life is atoning. So salvation extends to the totality of the human: the personal, the social, the sexual, and the spiritual.[52] Therefore, love cannot escape the vicarious humanity of Christ. Human beings must know their limit, as Adam did not, but not without recognizing that God is at the center of life, including the acts of love, not just the boundaries of definition and limits (Bonhoeffer).[53] How can God be both the center and the limit, however? The vicarious humanity of Christ describes both One who is at the center, since his substitution for us is total, and the One who represents us as the true human who realizes one's limit. Without Christ, God is not at the center and we do not realize our limit. Because of the vicarious humanity of Christ, we can say with Bonhoeffer, "God is at once the boundary and the center of our existence."[54] Not loving the other is only to hate the limit.[55] God at the center means that our hope is in the objectivity of Christ's victory over death, not in our subjectivity.[56] There are limits forced upon us by both our finitude and fate, yet God's mighty acts, ultimately in Christ's vicarious life and work, are not simply

---

51. Anderson, *On Being Human*, 177–78.
52. Anderson, "Theological Anthropology," 89.
53. Bonhoeffer, *Letters and Papers*, 366–67.
54. Bonhoeffer, *Creation and Fall*, 86.
55. Bonhoeffer, *Creation and Fall*, 99.
56. Alan E. Lewis, *Between Cross and Resurrection*, 430.

the answers to life's questions, but at the center of life itself. Alan Lewis says it well:

> We face suffering, distress, and death with courage, faith, and trust, not by maintaining serenity of psyche or buoyancy of soul within, but precisely by casting ourselves in all the times of emptiness, aridity, and wordlessness—as well as those still more spiritually dangerous times of optimism or elation—upon the gift of grace outside us and around us. God promises to do what we cannot do, and go where we need not go, to enter the dark valley ahead of us and defeat on our behalf the frightening foe.[57]

"God promises to do what we cannot do"! The undulation, the times of emptiness and then optimism is where the vicarious love of Christ can work, doing what we cannot do. In this way, the power of God works without overpowering our free will, as C. S. Lewis comments: "He cannot ravish. He can only woo," commending undulation as a natural part of life.[58] Genuine community, therefore, is not on its own, so desperate for power and meaning that it reverts to seeking its own transcendence or *telos* or becoming dependent upon an ideology or cause.[59]

The Son and the Love of the Father

In the midst of the undulation, in the midst of the *hominum confusionis* is the Son who articulates for us the love of the Father, the love that has become known, despite the "presence-amid-absence." The first movement of the incarnation is God coming to humanity as a human being. There is knowledge of God in the humanity of Jesus Christ. The "mystery" of Christ as divine and human points to an objective reality that is nonetheless inexhaustible: how God is known in the humanity of Christ and through his solidarity, therefore, with all of humanity.[60] Thus, according to Torrance, "Jesus Christ is Himself the Sacrament . . . for it is in Him that the One Truth of God comes to us in creaturely form and existence, so that in the

---

57. Alan E. Lewis, *Between Cross and Resurrection*, 430–31.
58. C. S. Lewis, *The Screwtape Letters*, 37–38.
59. Kettler, *Breadth and Depth of the Atonement*, 121.
60. T. F. Torrance, *Theological Science*, 149.

Is Love Essential to Our Humanity?

objectivity of His particular and historical humanity we encounter the eternal objectivity of God Himself."[61]

Two Movements of the One Incarnation

If *the first movement* of the incarnation ("humanward," as we have called it) is solidarity with humanity, to the point of the cross, *the second movement* (referred to as "Godward") is a response of love for the Father, a demonstration of what it truly means to be human, in the vicarious humanity of Christ. Jesus is the basis, first, of our language to God. "The real text of the New Testament Scriptures is the humanity of Christ. He is God's exclusive language to us and He alone must be our language to God," Torrance can say.[62] Even in lamenting, Jesus does what we are unable to do: simultaneously possess despair and joy, presence and absence, because he also knows the love of the Father. The Son knows the love of the Father, even in the midst of the descent into hell for us. That is why he responds on our behalf and in our place with love to the Father. In the humanity of the Son we see what it means to be human: to respond to the Father with love, based on the Father's love, in the Spirit, and not just to the Father, but for others as well.

The Vicarious Response of Christ

The vicarious response of Christ is both faith and love. They are different. They are two of the three things that "abide," along with hope (1 Cor 13:13). The "greatest," of course, is love. Is not Christ's response for us, his vicarious response, both a response of faith in and love for the Father, both which we need tremendously? In fact, in his life, we see faith and love seamlessly blend, which should be the goal of the Christian life as well, of course. Perhaps Nygren is right to view faith as "the whole devotion of love" in the context of a "reciprocated love," that is, the response of the love given by the Father.[63] The Son knows that. We really do not.

This response is a *vicarious* response, on behalf of and in the place of, the response of a friend, perhaps the greatest love, as we have suggested. God is known as a friend in Jesus. You are no longer servants, Jesus said,

---

61. T. F. Torrance, *Theological Science*, 150.
62. T. F. Torrance, *God and Rationality*, 151.
63. Nygren, *Agape and Eros*, 127.

but "I have called you friends" (John 15:15). For God to be our friend, Barth contends, means that humanity has value because "God sets value on him," not because of humanity's achievements and products, as much as these achievements and products might be needed.[64] Jesus differentiates the "servant" from the "friend" because "the servant does not know what the master is doing" (John 15:15a). Therefore, it is understood that to be a "friend" of God is to know what the master is doing, not to be ignorant of his ways, just as the mutual knowledge between the Father and the Son is not known except by the disclosure by the Son (Matt 11:27; Luke 10:21). This disclosure, however, is not just of *Heilsgeschichte*, salvation history, but a genuine knowledge of both God and humanity. It is not the ministry of Christ if humanity is only seen in relation to God or God only in relation to man. That does not sound very pious! Should not we always view humanity in relation to God? But Barth may be thinking here of pre-Renaissance medieval Europe and the virtue of the Renaissance in studying humanity for humanity's sake, not just so we can know about God from the study of humanity. We should be allowing "the mode of rationality" that is distinctive to human beings (T. F. Torrance) (as there is a "mode of rationality" distinct to God) to be respected if God is truly a friend to humanity.

In Jesus Christ, God finds us as "ordinary" people, yet makes ordinary people into new people.[65] The Son of God is not afraid to become "the Bearer of human mediocrity and triviality," and to go into the depths of our humanity, for he knows that he will be exalted, and take humanity with him. Here is the "double grace" of justification and sanctification (Calvin).[66]

As a friend, God does not simply want to "use" human beings for his purposes (Augustine's *uti* and opposed to *frui*, enjoyment).[67] Friendship love accepts the other for what one is, not how the friend can be "used." As such, God as friend means that God works *vicariously*, on the behalf of humanity. He is the friend who will be our advocate when no one else is (Ps 18:3, 6; 1 John 2:1). For God to be our friend means that God as friend has already been recognized by God in his response to the Father as the Son. There is no anxiety or burden in human hearts that they may or may not respond, or that the response may or may not be right. God as friend does demand a response of friendship in return, yet the basis for humanity's

---

64. Barth, *CD* IV/3.2, 800.
65. Barth, *CD* IV/2, 392–93, 396.
66. Calvin, *Institutes*, 3.11.1.
67. Augustine, *On Christian Teaching*, 16–17. Cf. Elshtain, *Who Are We?*, 53.

Is Love Essential to Our Humanity?

response of friendship to God is the perfect response of friendship by the Son to the Father. Jesus can call the disciples friends because *he knows first* what it means to be a friend of God.

This vicarious response of Christ has Christ already taking a place ahead of us, but not without our humanity.[68] This is a place where Christ does not rest but "strides through the ages," where the Christian is called to stand with him, in fellowship with him, in a true "liberation" more dynamic than "freedom." This kind of freedom moves one from the worlds of "desire" and "demand" into that of "receiving," just as the Son receives from the Father.[69] The "differentiation" in the Triune God is the very source of this receiving, a differentiation that demonstrates its own beauty in grace, grace in both creation and redemption, but ultimately as mirrors of the eternal Holy Trinity. This is "God's one life of joy."[70] Receiving is not foreign to the Triune God, nor to the vicarious humanity of Christ in his relation to the Father. Nor should it be to our humanity through the Spirit. Thus receiving is much more fundamental to our humanity than even diversity. This is the common humanity that has been assumed by Christ, not primarily our diversity but our common humanity that transcends all cultures.[71] This should sound a warning to our culture which too easily impoverishes itself with "diversity," particularly in education as one of the sole values (along with "tolerance"). Love, in all of its trinitarian richness, can be easily left behind.

This response by Christ with our humanity involves the humanity of others as well, "the community of saints."[72] One, therefore, is not meant to suffer and die alone. The church is the place of the vicarious humanity of Christ in the concrete sense that Bonhoeffer found lacking in Barth's theology.

Above all, Jesus Christ brings to light "the new man . . . the exalted and true man," who is now our truth.[73] Human recalcitrance cannot alter this fact, "what the man Jesus is for us, and for all men, the freedom of his knowledge of God."[74]

---

68. Barth, *CD* IV/3.2, 663.
69. Barth, *CD* IV/3.2, 668–69.
70. Hart, *Beauty of the Infinite*, 185–86.
71. Anderson, *Emergent Theology*, 154.
72. Bonhoeffer, *Sanctorum Communio*, 180.
73. Barth, *CD* IV/2, 300–301.
74. Barth, *CD* IV/2, 410.

Human Relationships and Distinctiveness

This love will be similar to human relationships. Distinctiveness is not obliterated but rather created in the mutual indwelling of relationships. Adam did not know himself as an individual until he met Eve. In contrast to our later western individualism, he did not even know what it means to be an individual until he existed with Eve in "co-humanity."[75] In Martin Buber's words, "I require a You to become; becoming I, I say You . . . All actual life is encounter."[76] This is counter to the belief that we "actualize" ourselves. Quite in contrast, this individuality comes from without, an opening to understanding the vicarious humanity, who comes to us in the midst of our impossibilities, not possibilities.[77] Perhaps we can say with Anderson that every human encounter is a search for co-humanity.[78] Even in the Trinity, we may say that the genuine distinctiveness of the persons of the Trinity is known in their mutual encounter.[79] The oneness of God does not deny distinctiveness. Our experience may be that each person takes responsibility for oneself; but even that can be a lie. Are we not what we are because of relationships with others?[80] That the Son is of "same substance/essence/being" with the Father (the *homoousion* of the Nicene Creed) nevertheless speaks of a differentiation as well.[81] The *homoousion* certainly bears witness "that what God is toward us in Jesus Christ and in his Spirit he is inherently and eternally in himself."[82] We read "something" from God in the "economy," Torrance claims, into who God is in himself. Might that differentiation in God include especially a relationship of love, the relationship between the Father and the Son in the Spirit? Certainly "apophatic reserve" is needed as we realize the limitations of creaturely language about God.[83] This does not mean that God is other than what he has revealed himself to be, Torrance hastens to add. But is it right to say that the "ultimate truth" of God, even though we call God "father" and "son," "is

---

75. Anderson, *On Being Human*, 44–50.
76. Buber, *I and Thou*, 62.
77. Anderson, *On Being Human*, 48.
78. Anderson, *On Being Human*, 50.
79. Fiddes, *Participation in God*, 243.
80. Smail, "Can One Man Die For All the People?," 78.
81. Colyer, *How to Read T. F. Torrance*, 235.
82. T. F. Torrance, *Trinitarian Perspectives*, 133–35.
83. T. F. Torrance, *The Christian Doctrine of God*, 159.

Is Love Essential to Our Humanity?

hidden in the mystery of God's transcendent being"?[84] Is that an unforced Kantian or Platonism that has crept into Torrance's thinking here? *Genuine* knowledge is not the same as *exhaustive* knowledge. We may not know God *exhaustibly*, but we may still know God *truly*. When Adam's differentiation finally happens, when Eve is created, he finally knows himself truly (Gen 2:23). Yes, Barth can say, "we do not know what we are saying when we call God Father and Son."[85] We allow God to define these words for us. His being known in his act (Matt 11:25-27). Therefore, Barth can also say, "It is not true that in some hidden depth of His essence God is something other than Father and Son."[86]

In addition, in the persons of the Trinity, there is not just static existence, but the mutual indwelling of love, the *perichoresis* of the Fathers.[87] Again, this is a place for the economy to lead us back to the eternal relations in God himself. Torrance cites the *perichoresis* as both teaching that the economic Trinity points to who God is inherently and eternally within himself, a relationship of love, as well as speaking of "a truth about the intimate relations in the divine Life which we cannot but formulate in fear and trembling" since, by God's "gracious condescension" it signifies "realities beyond themselves."[88] The limits of languages genuinely point beyond themselves, just as Holy Scripture points beyond itself to Christ. Scripture itself is incapable of giving definition to God, as Barth points out, cited by Torrance: "In our hands even terms suggested by Holy Scripture will prove to be incapable of grasping what they are supposed to grasp."[89] This does not mean that the real God is unknowable. For Barth prefaces this statement, admitting that even though "we cannot define the Father, the Son, and the Holy Spirit," the three persons have the freedom to "delimit themselves," for knowledge of God comes by God's grace, even in our interpretation of Holy Scripture. "What has to be said will obviously be said definitely and exclusively by God Himself, the three in the one God who delimit themselves from one another in revelation."[90]

---

84. T. F. Torrance, *The Christian Doctrine of God*, 159.
85. Barth, *CD* I/I, (Second Edition), 433.
86. Barth, *CD* I/I, (Second Edition), 432.
87. T. F. Torrance, *Christian Doctrine of God*, 172.
88. T. F. Torrance, *Christian Doctrine of God*, 173.
89. Barth, *CD* I/1, (Second Edition), 476. Cited by T. F. Torrance, *Christian Doctrine of God*, 173.
90. Barth, *CD* I/1, (Second Edition), 476.

In the encounter of persons, however, there is not only joy but also despair. We cannot avoid weeping with another as much as we cannot avoid rejoicing with one another. So Paul can say of the body of Christ, "If one member suffers, all suffer together with it: if one member is honored, all rejoice together with it" (1 Cor 12:26. Cf. Rom 12:15). We must at times *vicariously* suffer for one another. The greatest sorrows should not be suffered alone. That is what it means to be true friends.

The encounter with one another means to result in friendship. For Jesus, this is no mere sharing of mutual interests: "No one has greater love than this, to lay down one's life for one's friends" (John 15:13). Yet Jesus does not stop there. He continues: "You are my friends if you do what I command you" (John 15:14). Atonement involves the intertwining of the life of Jesus personally with the lives of people.[91] This is where many theories of the atonement have failed to include the incarnate life and teachings of Jesus, such as Jesus making friends. His "distinctiveness" has led to friendship. Friends of Jesus follow him into his destiny, that of sacrificial death. This is that which seems not to engender belief, but unbelief. Ironically, the death of Jesus, bringing a "presence-amid-absence," that is, a crucified messiah, the stumbling block to Jews and folly to the gentiles, is God becoming one of them to the point of death.[92] The vicarious humanity of Christ shares in our humanity even to the point of death and burial, as difficult as it is for believer and non-believer alike to accept. For this is where humanness is revealed, Alan Lewis reminds us, in all of its transience, perishability, and weakness, a place where it is thought that God cannot and will not go.[93] The God revealed in Jesus Christ bursts these preconceptions apart. God is to be identified with the buried man of Nazareth. Then I can have hope for my wretched humanity. To love one another, to love a friend, to love another one with whom Christ shares his terminal humanity of death, is to be involved in his destiny, a destiny that one cannot escape. We are on the same boat together. A "difference" occurs in that there is another one, the neighbor, who is not Christ but nonetheless with whom he is in solidarity.[94] However, Jesus is with us. He is with us, in solidarity, but he is not kept to the same fate we are. He will not stay on the boat. He will not stay in the grave.

---

91. T. F. Torrance, *Atonement*, 161–62.
92. Alan E. Lewis, *Between Cross and Resurrection*, 91.
93. Alan E. Lewis, *Between Cross and Resurrection*, 92.
94. Barth, *CD* I/2, 435.

Distinctiveness and the World

However, this love will be distinct, at least in some ways, from the world, because the Son's response to the Father, even as friend, is unlike anything we know. The world, of course, knows sacrifice and devotion, Kierkegaard reminds us.[95] We often claim to be misunderstood, especially when that is blended with love.[96] Not only "ungodliness" collides with Christ but also "misunderstanding." Christ was the most misunderstood person of all time, yet he demonstrates nonetheless what it means to love God. His love for the world emphasizes the distinction between God and the world. However, this is not a distinction that means aloofness. Rather the kind of distinctiveness that means love.[97] Love is not restricted to union, but blossoms in terms of distinctiveness (Adam only was truly human when Eve, his "distinctiveness" was created!).[98] The vicarious response of the Son speaks of that answering to the Father's love reflecting a distinctiveness eternally in God, and in which we yearn for a humanity that desires to be truly human.

---

95. Kierkegaard, *Works of Love*, 109.
96. Kierkegaard, *Works of Love*, 110.
97. Hart, *Beauty of the Infinite*, 181–83.
98. Anderson, *On Being Human*, 44–54.

CHAPTER SIX

Where Are the Fruits of Love?

"Sheer Action" as the Fruit of Love

Love is known by "sheer action," Kierkegaard argues. (Perhaps it is silly that one should even "argue" for "action"! Well, SK was always known for irony!) "Disembodied love" is not real love, Ray Anderson contends.[1] It is known by its fruit. The biblical testimony that "love builds up" (1 Cor 8:1) is not to mean a coercive act. Love builds up, so it does not bulldoze or demand; "Love expects nothing, because it has reached the goal already" (Barth).[2] Love as an end, not as a means is a kind of "realized eschatology," not just holding down for the future. It must presuppose that love already exists in the other and not try to create it.[3] No, building up another in love means controlling oneself, not trying to control another.[4] However, Kierkegaard interestingly claims that the source of this fruit is "the hidden life of love."[5] In doing so, he brings us back to something more than just "sheer action": to the question of need. We need to love and to be loved. We need community. However, the greatest need may be to become self-giving. So *agape* ("gift-love") and *eros* ("need-love") must come together. We need the vicarious humanity of Christ in the life of the church, in the life of the community bound together by Christ.

1. Anderson, *Historical Transcendence*, 227.
2. Barth, *Epistle to the Romans*, 496.
3. Kierkegaard, *Works of Love*, 216.
4. Kierkegaard, *Works of Love*, 217.
5. Kierkegaard, *Works of Love*, 10.

Where Are the Fruits of Love?

Yet it can be very presumptuous when love presupposes love is in the other person.⁶ We are only too tempted for that to happen. Only the Son can presume that of the Father. That is why we need the vicarious love of the Son. We cannot and should not presume upon the love of another, as much as we need to love and want to be love. This "sheer action" of love is originally an eternal trinitarian reality within God, the opposite of a disembodied love, love that is only an ideal, a romantic illusion at best, a psychotic dysfunction at worst. In contrast is a love that can "believe all things" (1 Cor 13:7) with the Son, and make his love more embodied all the time, in his body and in the world, as erring and misguided as it is.⁷ That love does not live merely by the empirical, but as it is deepened daily by the trust of the Son of God.

A Need Fulfilled?

Is the need to love and to be loved a joy of life or a curse? And is it truly divine love if it simply satisfies a need? Is there a need in the triune God to love, or is love eternally a choice, even in God, especially as expressed in the incarnate response of love to the Father by the Son, done for us and in our behalf, in a vicarious way? A poet may have a need to write or the young woman, Kierkegaard says, a need to love. In fact, "the only real pauper" is the one "who went through life and never felt a need for anything!"⁸ Augustine's "restless heart" whose need is never satisfied until it finds its rest in God is never far behind our thinking.

A need is found when one knows the trustworthiness of the one who is loved. The Son knows that in the Father. Even if the Son doubts in Gethsemane or on the cross, the love by which he is loved is greater than any doubt he might have. Love does not fear doubt, Ray Anderson reminds us, for it does not spring from reason but from reality, where love says to "doubt love if it dare!"⁹

Jesus Christ reveals God truly, although in human flesh; he is not just a Halloween costume that speaks of God. Torrance's words are unforgettable: "God's revelation is identical with himself in the oneness and differentiation of God within his own eternal Being as Father, Son, and Holy

6. Kierkegaard, *Works of Love*, 219.
7. Kierkegaard, *Works of Love*, 221.
8. Kierkegaard, *Works of Love*, 10.
9. Anderson, *Soulprints*, 72.

Spirit, for what God is toward us in his historical self-manifestation in the Gospel as Father, Son, and Holy Spirit, he is revealed to be inherently and eternally in himself."[10] Torrance seems to allow for no wiggle room here; The "historical self-manifestation" in Jesus Christ reveals the eternal God. However, he will have a caveat. Yes, the *homoousion* itself of the Nicene Creed theologically tells us "that what God is antecedently, eternally, and inherently in himself he is indeed toward us in the incarnate economy of his saving action in Jesus Christ on behalf."[11] Since the Son is of the "same substance" as the Father, his incarnation reveals the divine Godhead. Immanence of the incarnation is no barrier to divine revelation. Both the *homoousion* of the Son and the mission of Spirit from the Father through the incarnate Son "have an essential place within the very life of God."[12] Yet this revelation also reveals that there is a mystery, a limitation, so that one may not read back "temporal and causal connections" of creaturely existence or what is "human and finite" into divine being, otherwise this would be a "mythological projection of ideas" unto God.[13] In a way, this would be reading a kind of "natural theology" back into God. The oneness between the Son and the Spirit allows a "signitive, not mimetic" relationship, not one that reads back into God "material and creaturely images."[14] By "signitive" I take Torrance to mean the "sign" that points beyond it, the "witness" common in Torrance's theology that refers beyond itself, in contrast to the *mimesis,* the mimicking, identifying, such as identifying the words of the Bible with God himself, as does rationalistic fundamentalism, a frequent target of criticism in Torrance's writings.[15]

A mimetic approach (see Aristotle) might be expected, even welcomed, as a way to involve a genuine "human-Godward" response to the "God-humanward" initial movement of divine revelation of love in Jesus Christ. Should we not imitate God's love in Christ? Is this not the *imitatio Christi*? Yet this is where the vicarious humanity of Christ steps in and rules out our audacity in such an independent response.[16]

10. T. F. Torrance, *Christian Doctrine of God*, 1.
11. T. F. Torrance, *Christian Doctrine of God*, 97.
12. T. F. Torrance, *Christian Doctrine of God*, 99.
13. T. F. Torrance, *Christian Doctrine of God*, 97.
14. T. F. Torrance, *Christian Doctrine of God*, 101.
15. T. F. Torrance, Review of B. B. Warfield, 104–8; *Ground and Grammar of Theology*, 36; *Reality and Evangelical Theology*, 10, 16ff, 61, 68.
16. T. F. Torrance, *Christian Doctrine of God*, 106.

Where Are the Fruits of Love?

What we are involved in is "active participation" in "the kingdom and fatherly providence of God," yet not as a "co-creator" or "second Jesus Christ."[17] We are only to "follow" as a "recipient," as "the witness of Jesus Christ," in Barth's words. "Follow" is easy to say, but perhaps the vicarious humanity of Christ allows only the picture of one literally walking behind Jesus (as a Kansan, I am partial to the exhortation given to Dorothy in *The Wizard of Oz*: "Follow the yellow brick road!"). We have no path of our own, no place of our own, only as the "recipient." Yet this is a very active walk we are involved in, because Jesus Christ is still "walking" in this world, in the church, through the Spirit.

However, is this only true if God has *chosen* these "temporal and causal connections" to communicate who he is? Truly, they are unable to communicate exhaustively who God is. And, like any analogy, they fail at points. Much more, that is true with God. Nevertheless, just because these connections are not exhaustively true does not mean they are insufficient. Torrance himself often draws the distinction between our ability to *apprehend* God, because of revelation, versus an ability to *comprehend* God.[18] We will never be able to comprehend the eternal, infinite God of the universe; but we can apprehend what we are given to be known by his grace; and what we know first is *relational*, the relations between the Father and the Son in the Spirit, the love of the Godhead. That love, however, may surprise us. It may, for example, include "obedience," "worship," even "faith," all actions of the Son towards the Father, in response to the Father's love. We must be careful, of course, not to read our ideas of love into the divine, triune love, but, nevertheless, to be taught what divine love is. Of course, this is a challenge!

Jesus Christ himself, Torrance contends, as "the one and only Form and Image of God given to us" is "the crucial point of reference" that will "filter away" from our conceiving of God "all that is inappropriate or foreign to him such as, for example, sexual relations or distinctions in gender which by their nature belong only to creaturely beings."[19] The incarnation means that the creator became the creature. This was in the context of Jesus Christ being a male. It is not hard to see his gender, however, as incidental to the revelation of God in Jesus Christ. In addition, is Torrance helpful when he speaks of the coordination of the *homoousion* of the Son with the *homoousion* of the Spirit as a criterion? In what way? He is not

---

17. Barth, *CD* III/4, 482.
18. Barth, *CD* III/4, 26.
19. Barth, *CD* III/4, 107.

specific. However, when he continues to speak of the relation between "the homoousial oneness between the economic Trinity and the transcendent Trinity," on the one hand, with "the doctrine of the perichoretic relations within the eternal Communion of the Father, the Son and the Holy Spirit," he provides much more promise. For the *perichoresis* speaks of the "mutual indwelling" of *love* between the persons of the Trinity. A criterion can truly exhibit a relationship of love between the Father and the Son in the Spirit where the economic relationship can reflect the eternal, transcendent, immanent, ontological being of God. The "obedience" of the Son (not understood exclusively in terms of our experience of "obedience," however), may be one example. The Son responds to the Father's love with obedience, an obedience of love that is subordination without inferiority, along with faith, service, and worship, through the vicarious humanity of Christ. It seems to me that this is not difficult to affirm.

We can only approach the eternal, ineffable being of God with fear and trembling, rushing to the vicarious humanity of Christ in his priesthood and mediation, realizing that the only way to know God in a "godly" way is through "godly ways of thought and speech." This is the way of worship, and Christ the High Priest (Hebrews) best exemplifies that way.[20] It is the place of the Spirit of God to enable us to participate in Christ's high priestly ministry. As Christ intercedes for us, the Spirit intercedes, and helps us to pray in our weakness.[21] This is the same Holy Spirit by which Jesus was born and baptized, and through him he offered himself to the Father (Rom 8:34; Heb 7:25).[22] The eternal love between the Father, the Son, and the Holy Spirit poured itself into Jesus of Nazareth, and therefore into our lives. The fruit of love is found in our participation in this eternal life of love.

The result of Athanasius's crusade for the *homoousion* doctrine was to bring forth a unity between the Father and Son, and unity of love versus the separation found in Arius's doctrine. Arius might claim that the ontological distinction between the Father and the Son would argue more strongly for love, but the *homoousion* enabled Athanasius to bring love into the being of God, the being in God known in God's acts, as the Torrances put it. Love is therefore essential to who God is. The vicarious humanity of Christ, therefore, that man-Godward act, reflects that which is eternal in God, a

---

20. Barth, *CD* III/4, 110–11. Cf. Athanasius in his *Orations against the Arians*.
21. T. F. Torrance, *Incarnation*, 136.
22. T. F. Torrance, *Incarnation*, 137.

Where Are the Fruits of Love?

response of love to love. That is the essential fruit and the basis for all future fruits of love.

Love continues to grow. The Father is not the Father without the Son, the very basis for mutual indwelling, the communion of *perichoresis*.[23] Each person of the Trinity retains his individuality, in a union without confusion. *Perichoresis* upholds, and does not destroy, distinctiveness. Reciprocity establishes distinctiveness.[24] Yet it is a love from all eternity. The strongest words in the Synoptic Gospels for the unity of being between the Father and the Son ("no one knows the Son except the Father and no one knows the Father except the Son . . .) (Matt 11:27) are followed immediately by the Son imploring his audience to "Come to me, all you that are weary and are carrying heavy burdens, and I will give you rest (Matt 11:28). *"I will give you rest."* He is able, in his vicarious humanity, to give us something we plead for: rest. "Rest" from the "heavy burdens," whatever they may be, may be one of the greatest gifts of love that can be given.

Yet that "rest" is not apart from community. "Take my yoke upon you" continues Jesus (Matt 11:29). We are invited to a new labor or "yoke," to join in the community of Jesus.[25] The fruit of love then can be found in reciprocal relations, in *community*. That is both the means and the goal to which we are heading. The fruit of love, in other words, is eschatological. We may be in loneliness now (Kierkegaard!), but we are heading towards community, even as we imperfectly experience community now (Why do the monks always seek a monastery?).

The One Purpose of God's Love

Yet, Jesus Christ manifests to us God's love in a particular form: As John McLeod Campbell claims, the very nature of the incarnation is to declare the one purpose of God's love, including the Father who sends the Son.[26] Christ is trying to do nothing more and nothing less than to draw us to the Father in a life of communion.[27] This contrasts with the life of the "overgrasping self."[28] First Corinthians 13:3 speaks the "noble" actions, indeed

23. T. F. Torrance, *Incarnation*, 130, 132.
24. T. F. Torrance, *Incarnation*, 175.
25. T. F. Torrance, *Incarnation*, 135.
26. Campbell, *The Nature of the Atonement*, 20.
27. James B. Torrance, *Worship, Community and the Triune God of Grace*, 93.
28. Allison, *Night Comes*, 80.

"spiritual" and "moral" actions of giving away all of one's possessions (Jesus gave an exhortation "to sell" one's possessions at least more than once: Matt 19:21; Mark 10:21; Luke 12:33; 18:22). Yet this can be fruitless without love, says Paul. The one motive of real obedience is something that only Christ can provide.[29] Barth speaks of this as a witness to Jesus Christ, but should we not speak even more strongly of the vicarious humanity of Christ, who takes our place, and allows us to participate in his obedience, his witness?

The atonement, seen as the development of the incarnation (not separate from it, as is often the case), manifests this one purpose of love, not, as in many theories of the atonement, God attempting to reconcile justice and love. The cry on the cross is a part of the atonement and however "God-forsaken" it may be, it is still a "presence-amid-absence" (Alan E. Lewis), in which God is there in the midst of our hells. What "need" we have to be measured, Campbell continues, is not just our need "but by what God has done to meet our need."[30] This is in contrast to "the inadequate and superficial views of the gospel which so often give peace, even to minds considerably awakened on the subject of religion."[31] Our "need" may be for "peace," but it is only our conception of "peace." God's love will not let us be satisfied with that. We now can love what we have previously hated, since we now know of God's love.[32] We are now glad to have a Lord. This is what it means to enter into *theosis*, to become godly, to become conformed to the image of Christ, "to love what God loves, and therefore to do what God does."[33] We are freed from a life of "the nomistic form of human existence," a life burden with what Paul called "the curse of the law" (Gal 3:13), that which justification throws into a "sharp relief" as a life of "the irreversibility of guilty deeds and lives," imprisoning us behind the bars of necessity, deeds that can never be undone.[34]

The "one purpose of love," if it is *agape*, means to be indiscriminate, and therefore, lacking in taking into account special circumstances of compassion, for example, a particular social or ethnic group above others.[35]

---

29. Barth, *CD* I/2, 447.
30. Campbell, *Nature of the Atonement*, 21.
31. Campbell, *Nature of the Atonement*, 21.
32. Barth, *Knowledge of God*, 118.
33. Ziegler, "The Form of Formation," 353.
34. T. F. Torrance, *Space, Time and Resurrection*, 96–97. See also Nygren, *Agape and Eros*, 264.
35. Outka, *Agape*, 269.

Where Are the Fruits of Love?

We make discriminate choices every day, from where to live to whom we marry, or if we marry. Certainly, a definition of *agape* as "disinterested" love can encourage this. The "one purpose of love," however, seen in the vicarious humanity of Christ and expressed in the response of the Son to the Father has no concern for any special interest group but for "the world" God so loved with great interest (John 3:16). Worked out in the world, it begins with the love of the Son for the Father, fulfilling the law of God. This affects the neighbor, Paul says, "Love does no wrong to a neighbor; therefore love is the fulfilling of the law" (Rom 12:10). However, who has fulfilled the law for us in advance? Jesus Christ, who said, "I have come not to abolish but to fulfill (the law)" (Matt 5:17). He has done something more, Paul says, "apart from law," and has disclosed a new "righteousness of God" that is a gift of grace based on "the faith of (or in) Jesus Christ" (Rom 3:21–22). This is genuine "realized" eschatology (or rather "realizing" eschatology), but that has its fulfillment with a "new creation."

God's "Holy Sorrow" of Love

At this point, Campbell brings in the notion of God's "holy sorrow" as a predicate of God's love. In Bonhoeffer's early thought, "Christ-existing-as-church-community," confession of sins is where "God's own self is at work in the act of repentance."[36] This is an event of what God is in himself first, not of wrath, but of fellowship between the Father and the Son.[37] Because of this fellowship, God is in sorrow over our sin, over our plight. God's sorrow brings forth in the humanity of Christ a perfect confession of our sins, an "Amen from the depths of the humanity of Christ to the divine condemnation of his sin."[38] The Son is the one who says, "Yes, Father, you are right, and we respond with the confession of sin." The Son declares that on our behalf and in our place. To deal with death and corruption one needs stronger language to include physical death as well.[39] Attitude is not enough. Yet, decades later, in his *Atonement* lectures and in his last published work during his lifetime, *Scottish Theology*, Torrance acknowledges the power of the confession on Christ's soul. He now recognizes both the suffering of the

---

36. Bonhoeffer, *Sanctorum Communio*, 214. Cf. 293–94 on *Stellvertretung* ("vicarious representative action").
37. Barth, *CD* IV/2, 341.
38. Barth, *CD* IV/2, 118.
39. T. F. Torrance, *Doctrine of Jesus Christ*, 174.

Father, the "holy sorrow" and the suffering of the Son in his "perfect confession," because of their relationship of love. Christ's "vicarious penitence and sorrow" for our sins is a part of his wide ministry of vicarious humanity, beginning with his baptism in the Jordan, a baptism for repentance, as it was called (Luke 3:3).[40] This is a willing acceptance of the Father's judgment on our sin, an essential place for Christ's vicarious humanity in terms of judgment, yet also revealing the depths of vicarious confession or penitence as seen by Campbell. In the end, as Torrance wonderfully puts it, we go before the presence of God "not with our own confession but with Christ's confession as our true and only confession."[41]

All, in effect, have been shamed by Jesus, "the true man."[42] Jesus shames us in the right way, to bring us to confession of sin, because we have had a living encounter with him, not simply an idea or concept. We cannot, much to our chagrin, say that Jesus is God in order to write him off as being absolutely different from us. We share the same humanity. Not just at the point of death is he vicarious. However, since he is like us, not only do we share in his humiliation, we share in his exaltation (Phil 2:5–11). However, the shaming question may be asked of us, as it was of Peter, concerning our love for Jesus (John 21:17). This is all a part of the "bending our will back to agreement with the divine will . . . bringing our human mind back into agreement with the divine mind."[43]

Love as Sorrow / Sorrow as Repentance

Love is the motivation for sorrow and repentance, as seen in the story of the repentant woman (Luke 7:36–50). "Her sins, which are many, are forgiven, for she loved much" (Luke 7:47; cf. Matt 26:6–13; Mark 14:3–9; John 12:1). Love as sorrow is the motivation for penitence. The Word of God reveals that in "the self-knowledge of repentance" we have nothing to bring to God but to repent.[44] God has to intervene. Penitence is not a condition in order to be accepted by God, but as C. S. Lewis remarks, this is "simply a description of what going back to him is like."[45] The parable of the prodigal

---

40. T. F. Torrance, *Atonement*, 69–70.
41. T. F. Torrance, *Atonement*, 91.
42. Barth, *CD* IV/2, 386.
43. T. F. Torrance, *Atonement*, 70.
44. Barth, *CD* I/2, 390.
45. C. S. Lewis, *Mere Christianity*, 60.

son (Luke 15:11–32) may be more of a description of the atonement than many expect. In fact, as R. C. Moberly comments, love here is expressed as sorrow. Sorrow does not merely accompany love but love is expressed as sorrow for her sins.[46] However, perfect penitence is only possible for one who has not sinned.[47] As C. S. Lewis says, "Only a bad person needs to repent; only a good person can repent perfectly."[48]

In effect, Jesus "hated" his own life to the point of death because he acknowledged the Father's "holy sorrow."[49] Jesus commands us to give up our lives as he gave up his life. However, he does this, Lewis contends, by "helping" with our love and reason by God's love and reason, like a parent who holds the child's hands while the child is learning how to write.[50] By contrast, the slothful person is the one who hates God and wants to be free from him, the person of ingratitude, who does not love God.[51]

Is this adequate, however? Does God just hold our hands so we can love and reason? He does not just enable us (cf. John Cassian, Semi-Pelagianism, and John Wesley), but gathers us up with him to share in his love and reason, made manifest in love as sorrow for sins in the perfect Amen of the Son to the Father, the vicarious humanity of Christ. Lewis can speak of the need for God to become human and for us to share in "God's dying" but this process of "the perfect penitent" is only something we go through "if God does it in us." Saying "in us" is different from saying it is something God does *for* us, on our behalf and in our place. In fact, Lewis concludes that Christ as "the perfect penitent" is only a "picture." "Do not mistake it for the thing itself; and if it does not help you, drop it."[52] Why then, bring this up in a discussion of "mere" Christianity, which he defines as "what it is and was what it was long before I was born and whether I like it or not"?[53] Perhaps Lewis is more persuaded by the truth of the "perfect penitent," or the vicarious repentance of Christ, than he wants to admit. He certainly

---

46. Moberly, *Atonement and Personality*, 28.

47. Moberly, *Atonement and Personality*, 43, 117.

48. C. S. Lewis, *Mere Christianity*, 59.

49. Luke 14:26; Cp. Campbell, *Nature of the Atonement*, 215–16: "He had all along said, 'Father, into thy hands I commend my spirit.' In actual death He now said so . . . It is an utterance *in death*. He who thus puts trust in the Father is *tasting death* while doing so." Campbell takes the death of Christ seriously. Cf. 185–86.

50. C. S. Lewis, *Mere Christianity*, 60.

51. Barth, *CD* IV/2, 405.

52. Barth, *CD* IV/2, 61.

53. Barth, *CD* IV/2, 7.

celebrates Christ the "new man" as the next step in the evolution of humanity, which has already arrived.[54] Christ has taken our place. This "new man" offers an utterly new life to the Father, a communion of unbroken faith, obedience, and worship, a life of love that we cannot offer, but that now we can share in.[55]

The Entire Vicarious Humanity of Christ

John McLeod Campbell's doctrine of Christ's "perfect confession" of our sins needs to be interpreted as one aspect of the entire vicarious humanity of Christ, as James Torrance argues.[56] In a world of needless and pointless suffering, only the Son has the right to believe; only he has the right to call God Father.[57] He is the only One who answers, who can answer for us.[58] In him, he was converted for all of us.[59] This is not done to condition the Father into loving us, but a manifestation of the triune being of God as a communion of love, a different doctrine of God than one that is a doctrine more reflecting the influence of Aristotelian and Stoic concepts of natural law, Western jurisprudence, and post-Enlightenment thought.[60] R. C. Moberly, though not finding an "inclusive humanity" of Christ in Campbell, stresses Christ's identification with humanity as the basis of a "perfect penitence."[61] The entirety of the vicarious humanity of Christ is a picture of the "wondrous exchange" of the Fathers (2 Cor 8:9), and how deep and wide that is, as expressed by Gregory Nazianzen:

> Let us become like Christ, since Christ became like us. Let us become gods for
>
> his sake, since he for ours became man. He assumed the worse that he might
>
> give us the better; he became poor that we through his poverty might be rich;

---

54. Barth, *CD* IV/2, 62.

55. James B. Torrance, *Worship, Community and the Triune God of Grace*, 48.

56. James B. Torrance, "New Introduction," 11.

57. Bobrinskoy, *Compassion of the Father*, 104. See also Kettler, *The God Who Believes*, 132–65 on evil and suffering.

58. Barth, *CD* IV/1, 15.

59. Barth, *CD* IV/1, 131.

60. James B. Torrance, "New Introduction," 16.

61. Moberly, *Atonement and Personality*, 405–6.

took upon himself the form of a servant that we might receive back our liberty;

He came down that we might be exalted; he was tempted that we might conquer, he was dishonoured that he might glorify us; he died that he might save us; he ascended that he might draw to himself us, who were lying low in the fall of sin.[62]

"Becoming like Christ" is coming unto that union of love between the Father, Son, and the Spirit. However, it is not we who are doing the exaltation. We are exalted with Christ by God, with the vicarious humanity of Christ. That is the fruit of love, an actual act of substitution through exaltation, only because, first, there has been a humiliation.

Love as a Response by the One Who is Loved

Love is a response by one who is loved. T. F. Torrance dares to say, "Jesus Christ is our human response to God."[63] How outrageous that sounds! Is not a response, a faith and obedience to God on our part, a response to what Christ has done for us? So goes the popular theology. However, does this objection take seriously enough our desperate situation? Moreover, love is our most desperate need yet problem. Jesus' response to the Father is a response of love, the fruit of the love of God the Father. It becomes our response as we are united with him, our humanity united with the totality of his humanity. Jesus is both the Word of God spoken to humanity but also the Word heard by humanity.[64] In addition, what he hears is the love of the Father, a love we find at least difficult to hear, but often simply refuse to hear in its fullness, its judgment as well as grace. This is a Word, T. F. Torrance contends, that is heard not just from above, externally, but from within in us, because the Word of God in Jesus Christ has taken on our humanity and we are united with him. This personal union is the real basis of Christ's call for us to renounce ourselves, take up our cross, and follow him.[65] The foundation for all of this is that in this act of reconciliation (response) as well as of revelation in the incarnation, the being of God is revealed. The being of God is known in his act, as Barth and Torrance are fond of saying.

---

62. Gregory Nazianzen, *Discourse* I, 4, cited by Alfeyev, *Mystery of Faith*, 192.
63. T. F. Torrance, *Mediation of Christ*, 80.
64. T. F. Torrance, *Christian Doctrine of God*, 41.
65. T. F. Torrance, *Christian Doctrine of God*, 42.

This means nothing less than the communication of the "mutual indwelling" *(perichoresis)* between the Father and the Son in the Spirit, the essence of divine love. This "plenitude of personal being" in the triune God overflows to us in Christ, creating a "community of personal reciprocity in love, which we speak of as the Church living in the Communion of the Spirit."[66] The fruit of love proceeds from this eternal love, even if we cannot perceive its foundation with our senses. Faith is that which is "the assurance of things hoped for, the conviction of things not seen" (Heb 11:1). We do not see Jesus Christ now, Peter writes in his first epistle, yet his readers love him now, and even "rejoice with an indescribable joy" (1 Pet 1:8). Joy becomes the essence of love, even a fruit of love, even though Jesus Christ is not seen at this moment. Faith is knowledge, as Karl Barth reminds us.[67]

The Son responds in love to the Father because he knows he is already loved by the Father. This is our human response to God. We have no other. We have no other place to coerce God or to wonder if God loves us. We cannot be "clever" with God in our religious acts of spirituality or good deeds to think that we can earn God's love.[68] This is the story of all religions, is it not? In our cleverness, as a "deceiver" Kierkegaard would say, it is we who are surprised that we are loved by one who does not make any demand for reciprocal love apart from the Son who has already met that demand for us and in our place.

The "Last Adam" and the Love of God

The apostle Paul sees Christ as the one who takes the place of Adam. Adam is a broken mirror of Christ, whom Paul refers to as "the last Adam" (1 Cor 15:44–49), the final Adam because his origins are in heaven ("the man from heaven," 1 Cor 15:48–49). He is, in contrast to the first Adam, "a living giving spirit" (1 Cor 15:45). In Galatians Paul speaks of love as one of the fruits of the Spirit (Gal 5:22). So it should be no surprise that 1 Corinthians 13 (the "love" chapter) should be sandwiched between Paul's discussion of *the church* as the body of Christ in chapter 12 (especially relevant to that troubled Corinthian congregation) and the eschatology of Christ as the last Adam in chapter 15. In fact, an implicit Adam-Christ contrast may be in chapter 13: Love "does not insist on its own way" (1 Cor 13:4) as Adam

---

66. T. F. Torrance, *Trinitarian Perspectives*, 3.
67. Barth, *Dogmatics in Outline*, 22–27.
68. Kierkegaard, *Works of Love*, 240–41.

did, in contrast to Christ. Of course, the Corinthian church is more like Adam than Christ. Corinth was a community, but a distorted community that assumed they were already "kings," already "rich" (in contrast to Paul and his sufferings!) (1 Cor 4:8). The humanity of Christ is needed to take the place of the fallen humanity of Corinth. In this way humanity is set right back on the path to its original purpose.[69] Views of justification as mere rectification or "human rights" are found wanting in comparison with seeing justification as our participation in the active righteousness of Jesus given as a gift. Justification is the place Christ "has put himself in our place that we may be put in his place," the "wondrous" or "sweet" exchange (2 Cor 8:9).[70]

The last Adam is the final word about humanity because he is a heavenly word, "the man from heaven." He is "a life-giving spirit" (1 Cor 15:45) who breathes new life into others as the man of resurrection with "the power of an indestructible life" (Heb 7:16).[71] The resurrection of Christ is "the complete amen of the Son to the Father as of the Father to the Son."[72] Heaven should not be derided as an inferior destination, as it is by many moderns, even theologians, who prefer this vale of tears. It is with "the man from heaven" that "love abides" or "never ends" (1 Cor 13:8). The changeableness of human emotion, the passing of time, and the finitude of human love all challenge making such a statement: "love abides." It certainly does not on this earth, at least not always. Falling away from God is not the same as simply falling away from another lover; it is falling away from love.[73] Love can cease in erotic love and friendship love; the lover can wait for a long time, but then cease to wait. Has the lover really ever been loving then?[74] Divine love abides; it waits.

Love in/for the Community

In Wendell Berry's novel, *Jayber Crow*, the barber, Jayber, sees his little rural community of Port William in a new light when the love of God takes his place, "like a father with a wayward child, whom He can't help and can't

---

69. T. F. Torrance, *Atonement*, 131–32.
70. T. F. Torrance, *Atonement*, 134.
71. T. F. Torrance, *Atonement*, 217.
72. T. F. Torrance, *Atonement*, 228.
73. T. F. Torrance, *Atonement*, 304.
74. T. F. Torrance, *Atonement*, 303.

forget."[75] This is what it means for God to love the world (John 3:16). This love is so deep it assumes our nature. How God has loved makes everything secondary, including "belief." The community can become a community of love because it knows that it has already been loved. In this context we are reminded that the fruits of the Spirit ("love, joy, peace," etc.) are social.[76] That is where love becomes a reality. In the New Testament, the Spirit is not so much an aspect of inner psychology or creative spirituality as he is the "ecology," an environment, a place of genuine humanity, the humanity of Christ made manifest in our humanity.

The fruit of love, therefore, comes from an event in the life of God, an environment, an "ecology" in God himself. He takes on our humanity in order to confess perfectly on our behalf and in our place, doing something we are unable to do. At the heart of the matter is love as the essential attribute of God, not simply one among many.[77] Therefore, decretal Calvinists such as in the *Westminster Confession* and Jonathan Edwards can restrict the mercy and love of God to only the elect, not to all humanity. The fruit of love is possible because God is love. The Holy Spirit makes this double movement within God an event within us, enabling us to receive and understand this life.[78] John Gerstner can echo the beliefs of Jonathan Edwards and many others in saying "the greatest error of our times" in which "Jonathan Edwards never fell" is to say that "God is love" without saying he is "more than love and he is other than love. God is holiness; God is justice; God is wisdom; God is wrath."[79] Certainly, God is all those things. The biblical God is no impoverished God. However, the triune God whom Jesus knows is first the heavenly Father who loves him and whom he loves from all eternity in the Spirit. God has many attributes. However, all of those attributes (including justice) need to be read in light of the relationship to who God is: love. So we are called on to pray in the Spirit (Rom 8), knowing that in the Spirit there is a corresponding movement from God to our humanity and from humanity to God just as there was

---

75. Berry, *Jayber Crow*, 250–52.

76. Anderson, *An Emerging Theology*, 159, 164; T. F. Torrance, *Theology in Reconstruction*, 242.

77. Campbell, *Nature of the Atonement*, 73. Contra many conservative Protestant theologies, such as in Louis Berkhof, *Manual of Christian Doctrine*, 67.

78. T. F. Torrance, *Christian Doctrine of God*, 152.

79. Gerstner, *Jonathan Edwards*, 93. See a contrary view on heaven and hell in Allison, *Night Comes*, 93–150.

in the incarnation, indeed, as there is in the Father-Son relationship in the Spirit from all eternity.[80]

The fruit of love is first seen in one person, the one who is the God who loves and the man who loves God, the one in whom is both: Jesus Christ.[81] Herein the ancient christological controversies become important: Jesus Christ is not two persons but one, one person, and the hypostatic union, not to be confused, not to be separated (Chalcedon, AD 451). In contrast, we find it very difficult to both love and to be loved. In Jesus Christ, the covenant is kept from both sides, so he reveals the essential covenantal nature of both the being of God and the meaning of being human.

The very meaning of being human! The fruit of love says something important about being human, not just about God. This is not just an empty-headed religious euphoria about the betterment of things, nor a pessimistic downturn into despair and futility. Jesus Christ really has risen from the dead. Yet this means to confront world history only with love, not with fear or hate.[82] No other choice has been given us. Jesus Christ, in his vicarious humanity, has pushed aside any other alternative. The resurrection of Jesus from the dead is the resurrection of the one who has taken upon himself my humanity, in my place, on my behalf, at an ontological level, putting it to death on the cross, to death with its totality, not just behavior.[83] If the double movement of God in the vicarious humanity of Christ bears fruit in love, then reconciliation, not sin or sickness becomes the presupposition even for therapy, let alone for ministry. There is an "order of relations," to use Barth's and Bonhoeffer's terms, that we might call love between the Father and the Son in the Spirit, that precedes sin or sickness, which is the only thing that can bring forth genuine ministry or therapy. This order, Anderson contends, is *"belonging,"* a place where we can be healed, where "our believing is conditioned by our belonging" (Polanyi),[84] in contrast to any abstract idea or slogan. This is not easy because the church lives in the eschatological existence of the kingdom of God signified by the sacraments: they fall between the two ages where there is, nonetheless, a "real presence" of Christ today, yet in tension.[85] This is so that even in my death

---

80. See T. F. Torrance, *Christian Doctrine of God*, 152–53.
81. Barth, *CD* IV/3.2, 667.
82. Barth, *CD* IV/3.2, 717.
83. Anderson, *On Being Human*, 175.
84. Polanyi, *Personal Knowledge*, 322.
85. T. F. Torrance, *Atonement*, 260.

processional, when I am no longer under control, Ray Anderson suggests, the community of Christ acts vicariously for me.[86] This is part of the vicarious humanity of Christ.

The "Hidden" Source of Love

Love, indeed, for it to avoid superficiality, has a source, according to Kierkegaard, that is "hidden."[87] As the classic country rock group, The Band, put it, "There's no greater love than the love that dies untold."[88] One criticizes the heart that is "worn on the sleeve." It may lack depth or substance. Yet the love "that dies untold" ("hidden"!) bears its own fruit. (Is Kierkegaard thinking of his broken engagement to Regine?) This is a "work of love." This contrasts with those who might give to charity, visit the widow, or clothe the naked, but do so in "a self-loving way."[89]

Love has a true knowledge; it is not naive. It is a misinterpretation of the apostle to read, "love believes all things" (1 Cor 13:7) otherwise. Love knows the beloved so it is not involved in mistrust.[90] Yet there is much that is hidden from lovers. Kierkegaard says it plainly: "Is it not so that one person never completely understands the other?"[91]

Is this ultimate "hiddenness" in the love between the Father and the Son that which bears fruit in our salvation? Is that why the Gospels refuse to describe or picture Jesus (much less the Father and the Spirit!)? The economic Trinity in terms of Jesus' maleness, for example, should not be read into the Triune God. So also his race, his hair color, his language (God does not speak Aramaic), etc. As we have seen, Torrance speaks of these as "temporal or causal" or "material or creaturely images."[92] However, the economic Trinity (how God appears to us) is our only source for knowledge of the ontological or immanent Trinity (who God is in himself). The totality of the love between the Father and the Son is hidden. However, what we know is true, and it has been revealed to us in Christ. We only have the witness of Scripture about it. Therefore, we know the actions of

---

86. Anderson, *On Being Human*, 142–43.
87. Kierkegaard, *Works of Love*, 11.
88. The Band, "It Makes No Difference."
89. Kierkegaard, *Works of Love*, 13.
90. Kierkegaard, *Works of Love*, 228.
91. Kierkegaard, *Works of Love*, 229.
92. T. F. Torrance, *The Christian Doctrine of God*, 97, 101.

the Son that resulted from that love. (Is this the truth behind Augustine's *uti*, or "useful" love?) The cross, of course, could immediately be interpreted as something other than the result of love, if we did not know the testimony of the hidden love between the Father and the Son. We know it only because of the actions of faith, worship, service, and obedience by the Son in his earthly ministry on behalf of others, the vicarious humanity of Christ. These actions in obeying the Father's will are not outside the realm of the "tragic," (despite David Bentley Hart's protests. For him, there is no "pathos" in God).[93] As Ray Anderson reminds us, however, there is always something tragic about love, as long as there is some ontological differentiation between us. If nothing else, the beloved can always become absent from us.[94] Are we to retreat to a doctrine of God's *aseity* in order to resist these emotions in the triune God? Is there any other way to interpret the cry of abandonment, "My God, my God, why have you forsaken me?"[95] What we know about God's love, in other words is through the "sheer action" (Kierkegaard) of the vicarious *actions* of Christ. This is quite different from a sentimental message of love taught by a religious leader; how many often regard Jesus as that, even today. That is the danger of a view of incarnation without atonement, as one sees, for example in the writings of Richard Rohr.[96] He rightly rejects a view of atonement as that which tries to "buy off" God but fails to see the need for a sacrifice to be made, unlike the New Testament (Mark 10:45). Jesus, the "ransom for many," is not the basis for sentimental love, but a sacrifice because of the deep predicament in which humanity has found itself. Rohr and others seem not to see the importance of an ontological atonement that rescues humanity at its core through the vicarious humanity of Christ.

The need for such an ontological atonement is seen in humanity's "nomistic existence," as Torrance puts it, the "necessary" life that is under the law, burdened by guilt, under "the curse of the law" (Gal 3:13).[97] The "hidden" love between the Father and the Son through the Spirit that is now revealed in Jesus Christ, the one "born under the law" (Gal 4:4), demonstrates the depth of our problem in a way that no personal shaming or

---

93. Hart, *Beauty of the Infinite*, 166–67, 355, 357, 374–76.

94. Anderson, *On Being Human*, 177–78. Cf. on homosexuality and the tragic in Anderson, "Homosexuality," 266–83.

95. A. E. Lewis, *Between Cross and Resurrection*, 54.

96. Rohr, "Incarnation Instead of Atonement," 1.

97. T. F. Torrance, *Atonement*, 253.

soul searching ever could. Revealing our nomistic existence reveals our inability to save ourselves and the massive need for the vicarious humanity of Christ.[98]

Because of this "hidden" love, though it has become incarnate in Jesus Christ, the church is called to become uncommonly patient with its Lord in the world before the consummation of all things.[99] This is a life "between the times," in which "the violent" try to take the kingdom of God "by force" (Matt 11:12).[100] This is just the same as in Jesus' time, when he refused to force the time of the Father, despite others desiring him to force the issue.[101] He was always the faithful and obedient Son, on our behalf and in our place.

The church can only be patient in light of what it sees in the world because of the vicarious resurrection and ascension of Christ, as proclaimed by Peter on the day of Pentecost: "This Jesus God raised up, and of that all of us are witnesses. Being exalted at the right hand of God, and having received from the Father the promise of the Holy Spirit, he has poured out this that you both see and hear" (Acts 2:32–33). In this fusion of the resurrection and the ascension of Christ we have the continuing ministry of Christ, a ministry that is vicarious because he continues to act for us and in our place.[102] Christ continues to be apostle, priest, and king.

God as a Human Being, Not Just in a Human Being

These actions of God in Christ, while having implications at the core of our humanity, are also very particular actions, actions within the stuff of human history. God was revealed not just in a human being but as a human being, as T. F. Torrance likes to mention, referencing the Fathers.[103] Love can only be, therefore, particular actions of love, not a generic, sentimental, or abstract ideal. So, in *Jayber Crow*, the concrete love Jayber develops for Mattie, the woman he will never marry, and his church, even if it is not returned, becomes the occasion by which he can understand the love of God the Father in the Son. This is genuinely what it means to live by faith

---

98. T. F. Torrance, *Atonement*, 254.
99. T. F. Torrance, *Atonement*, 262.
100. T. F. Torrance, *Atonement*, 262.
101. T. F. Torrance, *Atonement*, 262–63.
102. T. F. Torrance, *Atonement*, 272.
103. T. F. Torrance, *Theology in Reconciliation*, 157. See also 135 and Kettler, *The Vicarious Humanity of Christ and the Reality of Salvation*, 122.

Where Are the Fruits of Love?

alone. What Jayber obtains is "love in my heart."[104] This love, the love of God for a world that does not love him, is a suffering love, the love that can break your heart (John 1:10–11).[105] Love can disappoint; love can fail. Our love can be thrown back at us in disregard. Is this not what leads to eternal damnation? We might become so "locked up in ourselves" that the light of God in Jesus is thrown back at God with such a force that "even the ultimate Love of God" becomes "a kind of hell for us."[106] The fruit of love, in other words, can be nothing less than suffering. We should not be surprised. The Father has "sorrow" for our sins, but that does not stop the Son going to the cross. What seems to be the failure of the Father in putting the Son on the cross is really the victory of the Son.[107]

Such a suffering love is a presence that does not need doubt. He never had any doubts, says T. F. Torrance of himself, not because of the brilliant logic of his theology, but because of his mother. A loving Christian family made knowledge of God "the most natural, intuitive thing of all."[108] Knowing God through Jesus Christ is concrete and particular, not because of any analogy of being, but because the fruit of that love is seen in loving relationships, of which the parent and the child is foremost to our humanity. The particular is the means by which we know the universal. In a biblical paradigm, the one is always the basis for blessing to the many, from Israel to the nations, to Jesus and all humanity.[109] We can live with the dialectic of joy and despair because, as Paul teaches, "the genuineness of your love" can even be expressed in the less than perfect Corinthian congregation through their concrete acts of love in helping to meet the needs of the Jerusalem church (2 Cor 8:8). He has a theological reason for believing this, as expressed in the next verse: "For you know the generous act (grace) of our Lord Jesus Christ, that though he was rich, yet for your sakes he became poor, so that by his poverty you might become rich" (2 Cor 8:9). Paul does not simply exhort the Corinthians to love; he points them to "the wonderful exchange" as the Fathers and John Calvin put it, in the double movement of love made manifest in the incarnation itself. The churches of Macedonia are

---

104. Berry, *Jayber Crow*, 247–54.
105. Berry, *Jayber Crow*, 254.
106. T. F. Torrance, *Transformation and Convergence*, 348.
107. Alan E. Lewis, *Between Cross and Resurrection*, 54–55.
108. Baumann, "Thomas F. Torrance," 111.
109. James B. Torrance, "The Vicarious Humanity of Christ," 137–41 and *Worship, Community and the Triune God of Grace*, 50–53.

The God Who Loves and Is Loved

an example to the Corinthians of those who have been objects of the grace of God in the midst of "a severe ordeal of affliction, their abundant joy, and their extreme poverty have overflowed in a wealth of generosity on their part" (2 Cor 8:1–2). The fruit of love is particular because the incarnation was a particular act of God's love.

Such love does not need doubt, yet it is not afraid of doubt either. Love exists because of reality, not doubt, as Ray Anderson claims, for love springs from reality, the particular, not from reason, our logical configurations.[110] Reality intervenes, as seen in the incarnation. Doubt has to deal with reality of love, as Jayber did in his love for Mattie. "We cannot know God behind his back," Torrance argues, "as it were, by stealing knowledge of him, for we may know him only in accordance with the way he has actually taken in revealing himself."[111] God is under no compulsion to reveal himself, but in his personal revelation in Christ, God presents us with a reality of love that makes a demand upon us because it is the demand of reality. For such love, faith is never far behind. How can one truly love without faith, without trust in the beloved? Such a love, such a faith, is what the Son has for the Father. This is the reality of the incarnation, a reality then made manifest in the church, when, in its most faithful times, it is "Christ existing as community," in Bonhoeffer's words, the body of Christ, in the world.

---

110. Anderson, *Soulprints*, 72.
111. T. F. Torrance, *Reality and Scientific Theology*, 201 n. 3.

Bibliography

Alfeyev, Hilarion. *The Mystery of Faith*. Edited by Jessica Rose. London: Darton, Longman, and Todd, 2002.
Allen, R. Michael. *The Christ's Faith: A Dogmatic Account*. New York: T. & T. Clark, 2009.
Allison, Dale C., Jr. *Night Comes: Death, Imagination, and the Last Things*. Grand Rapids: Eerdmans, 2016.
———. *The Sermon on the Mount: Inspiring the Moral Imagination*. New York: Crossroad, 1999.
Anderson, Ray S. *An Emergent Theology for Emergent Churches*. Downers Grove, IL: InterVarsity, 2006.
———. *Exploration into God: Sermonic Meditations on the Book of Ecclesiastes*. Eugene, OR: Wipf & Stock, 2006.
———. *Historical Transcendence and the Reality of God*. Grand Rapids: Eerdmans, 1975.
———. "Homosexuality: Theological and Pastoral Considerations." In *The Shape of Pastoral Theology*, 266–82. Downers Grove, IL: InterVarsity, 2001.
———. *The Gospel according to Judas*. Rev. ed. Colorado Springs: Navpress, 1994.
———. *Judas and Jesus: Amazing Grace for the Wounded Soul*. Eugene, OR: Wipf & Stock, 2005.
———. *On Being Human: Essays in Theological Anthropology*. Grand Rapids: Eerdmans, 1982.
———. *Self-Care: A Theology of Personal Empowerment and Spiritual Healing*. Wheaton, IL: Bridgepoint, 1995.
———. *Something Old, Something New: Marriage and Family Ministry in a Postmodern Culture*. Eugene, OR: Wipf & Stock, 2007.
———. *The Soul of God: A Theological Memoir*. Eugene, OR: Wipf & Stock, 2004.
———. "Theological Anthropology." In *The Blackwell Companion to Modern Theology*, edited by Gareth Jones, 82–94. Malden, MA: Blackwell, 2004.
———. *Soulprints: Personal Reflections on Faith and Love*. Huntington Beach, CA: Ray S. Anderson, 1996.
———. *Unspoken Wisdom: Truths My Father Taught Me*. Minneapolis: Augsburg Fortress, 1995.
Anselm. "Proslogion." In *A Scholastic Miscellany: Anselm to Ockham*. Edited by Eugene R. Fairweather, 69–93. New York: Macmillan, 1970.

Bibliography

Aristostle. *Introduction to Aristotle*. Edited by Richard McKeon. New York: Modern Library, 1947.

Augustine. *The City of God*. Translated by Henry Bettenson. London: Penguin, 1984.

———. *Confessions*. Translated by Henry Chadwick. Oxford: Oxford University Press, 1192.

———. *On Christian Teaching*. Translated by R. P. H. Green. New York: Oxford University Press, 1997.

Aulén, Gustav. *Christus Victor: An Historical Study of the Three Main Types of the Idea of the Atonement*. Translated by A. G. Hebert. New York: Macmillan, 1969.

The Band. "It Makes No Difference." *Northern Lights, Southern Cross*. Capitol Records. Written by Robbie Robertson, 1975.

Barbour, Ian. *Nature, Human Nature, and God*. Minneapolis: Fortress, 2002.

Barth, Karl. *Church Dogmatics* (cited as *CD*). Edited by Geoffrey W. Bromiley and T. F. Torrance. Translated by Geoffrey W. Bromiley, et al. 4 vols. in 14 parts. Edinburgh: T. & T. Clark, 1936–77.

———. *Dogmatics in Outline*. Translated by G. T. Thomson. New York: Philosophical Library, 1949.

———. *Epistle to the Philippians: 40th Anniversary Edition*. Translated by James W. Leitch. Louisville: Westminster/John Knox, 2002.

———. *Epistle to the Romans*. Translated by Edwyn C. Hoskyns. New York: Oxford University Press, 1933.

———. *The Knowledge of God and the Service of God*. Edited by J. L. M. Haire and Ian Henderson. Eugene, OR: Wipf & Stock, 2005.

———. *The Only Way: How Can the Germans Be Cured?* Translated by Marta K. Neufeld and Ronald Gregor Smith. New York: Philosophical Library, 1947.

———. *Theology and Church*. Translated by Louise Pettibone Smith. New York: Harper and Row, 1962.

Bauman, Michael, ed. "Thomas F. Torrance." In *Roundtable: Conversations with European Theologians*, 109–18. Grand Rapids: Baker, 1990.

Becker, Ernest. *The Denial of Death*. New York: Free Press, 1973.

Beilby, James, and Paul R. Eddy, eds. *The Nature of the Atonement: Four Views*. Downers Grove, IL: InterVarsity, 2006.

Berkhof, Louis. *Manual of Christian Doctrine*. Grand Rapids: Eerdmans, 1933.

Berry, Wendell. *Jayber Crow*. Washington, DC: Counterpoint, 2000.

Bobrinskoy, Boris. *The Compassion of the Father*. Translated by Anthony P. Gythiel. Crestwood, NY: St. Vladimir's Seminary Press, 2003.

Bonhoeffer, Dietrich. *Creation and Fall: A Theological Exposition of Genesis 1–3*. Dietrich Bonhoeffer Works 3. Edited by Martin Rüter et al. Translated by Douglas Stephan Bax. Minneapolis: Fortress, 2004.

———. *Discipleship*. Dietrich Bonhoeffer Works 4. Edited by Martin Kuske et al. Translated by Barbara Green and Reinhard Krauss. Minneapolis: Fortress, 2001.

———. *Ethics*. Dietrich Bonhoeffer Works 6. Edited by Ilse Tödt et al. Translated by Reinhard Krauss et al. Minneapolis: Fortress, 2005.

———. *Letters and Papers from Prison*. Dietrich Bonhoeffer Works 8. Edited by John DeGruchy. Translated by Isabel Best et al. Minneapolis: Fortress, 2010.

———. *Sanctorum Communio*. Dietrich Bonhoeffer Works 1. Edited by Clifford J. Green. Translated by Reinhard Strauss and Nancy Lukens. Minneapolis: Fortress, 1998.

Buber, Martin. *I and Thou*. Translated by Walter Kaufmann. New York: Scribner, 1970.

Bibliography

Calvin, John. *The Golden Booklet of the True Christian Life*. Translated by Henry van Andel. Grand Rapids: Baker, 2004.

———. *Institutes of the Christian Religion*. Edited by John T. McNeill. Translated by Ford L. Battles. Library of Christian Classics 20 and 21. Philadelphia: Westminster, 1960.

———. *Writings on Pastoral Piety*. The Classics of Western Spirituality. Edited by Elsie McKie. New York: Paulist, 2001.

Campbell, John McLeod. *The Nature of the Atonement*. Edinburgh: Grand Rapids: Eerdmans, 1996.

Clement of Alexandria. "The Rich Man's Salvation." In *From Christ to the World: Introductory Readings in Christian Ethics*, edited by Wayne G. Boulton et al., 451–52. Grand Rapids: Eerdmans, 1994.

Cochrane, Arthur. *Reformed Confessions of the Sixteenth Century*. Louisville: Westminster John Knox, 2003.

Colyer, Elmer M. *How to Read T. F. Torrance*. Downers Grove, IL: InterVarsity, 1999.

Cranfield, C. E. B. *Romans*. The International Critical Commentary 2. Edinburgh: T. & T. Clark, 1979.

Crisp, Oliver. "John McLeod Campbell and Non-penal Substitution." In *Retrieving Doctrine: Essays in Reformed Theology*, 92–115. Downers Grove, IL: IVP Academic, 2010.

D'Elia, John. *A Place at the Table: George Eldon Ladd and the Rehabilitation of Evangelical Scholarship*. Oxford: Oxford University Press, 2008.

Dostoevsky, Fyodor. *The Brothers Karamazov*. Translated by Richard Peavar and Larissa Volokhonsky. New York: Farrar, Strauss, and Giroux, 1990.

Dylan, Bob. "I Threw It All Away." *Nashville Skyline*. Columbia Records, 1969.

Fairweather, Eugene R., ed. *The Epistle to Diognetus*. Translated by Eugene R. Fairweather. In *Early Christian Fathers*, edited by Cyril R. Richardson, 205–24. Philadelphia: Westminster, 1970.

Farrow, Douglas. "T. F. Torrance and the Latin Heresy." *First Things* (December 1, 2013) 25–31.

Fiddes, Paul. *Participation in God: A Pastoral Doctrine of the Trinity*. Louisville: Westminister John Knox, 2000.

Ferreira, M. Jaimie. *Love's Grateful Striving: A Commentary on Kierkegaard's Works of Love*. Oxford: Oxford University Press, 2001.

Gerstner, John. *Jonathan Edwards on Heaven and Hell*. Grand Rapids: Baker, 1980.

Gillis, Chester. *A Question of Final Belief: John Hick's Pluralistic Theory of Salvation*. New York: St. Martin's, 1988.

Hart, David Bentley. *The Beauty of the Infinite: The Aesthetics of Christian Truth*. Grand Rapids: Eerdmans, 2003.

Helm, Paul. *The Providence of God*. Downers Grove, IL: InterVarsity, 1993.

Hick, John. *Evil and the God of Love*. 2nd ed. San Francisco: Harper and Row, 1977.

Horney, Karen. *Neurosis and Mental Health*. New York: Norton, 1950.

Hughes, Charles. "Pluralism, Inclusivism, and Christology." In *Jesus Then and Now: Images of Jesus in History and Christianity*, edited by Marvin Meyer and Charles Hughes, 154–69. Harrisburg, PA: Trinity, 2001

Irenaeus. *Against Heresies*. The Ante-Nicene Fathers, Vol. 1. Edited by Alexander Roberts and James Donaldson. Reprint. Grand Rapids: Eerdmans, 1950.

Kettler, Christian D. *The Breadth and Depth of the Atonement: The Vicarious Humanity of Christ in the Church, the World, and the Self*. Eugene, OR: Pickwick, 2017.

Bibliography

———. *The God Who Believes: Faith, Doubt, and the Vicarious Humanity of Christ.* Eugene, OR: Cascade, 2005.

———. *The God Who Rejoices: Joy, Despair, and the Vicarious Humanity of Christ.* Eugene, OR: Cascade, 2010.

———. *Reading Ray S. Anderson: Theology as Ministry, Ministry as Theology.* Eugene OR: Pickwick, 2010.

———. *The Vicarious Humanity of Christ and the Reality of Salvation.* Lanham, MD: University Press of America, 1991.

Kierkegaard, Søren. *Fear and Trembling.* Edited and translated by Howard V. Hong and Edna H. Hong. Princeton: Princeton University Press, 1980.

———. *Practice in Christianity.* Edited and translated by Howard V. Hong and Edna H. Hong. Princeton: Princeton University Press, 1991.

———. *Works of Love.* Edited and translated by Howard V. Hong and Edna H. Hong. Princeton: Princeton University Press, 1995.

Leith, John H. *John Calvin's Doctrine of the Christian Life.* Eugene, OR: Wipf & Stock, 2008.

Lewis, Alan E. *Between Cross and Resurrection: A Theology of Holy Saturday.* Grand Rapids: Eerdmans, 2001.

Lewis, C. S. *The Four Loves.* New York: Harcourt, Brace, Jovanovich, 1960.

———. *Mere Christianity.* New York: Macmillan, 1960.

———. *The Screwtape Letters.* New York: Macmillan, 1961.

———. *The Silver Chair.* NY: HarperTrophy, 1993 (1953).

———. *The Weight of Glory.* Grand Rapids: Eerdmans, 1965.

Marsden, George. *The Twilight of the American Enlightenment: The 1950s and the Crisis of Liberal Belief.* New York: Basic Books, 2014.

Moberly, R. C. *Atonement and Personality.* London: Murray, 1917.

Moltmann, Jürgen. *The Way of Jesus Christ: Christology in Messianic Dimensions.* Translated by Margaret Kohl. San Francisco: Harper San Francisco, 1990.

Molnar, Paul. *Divine Freedom and the Doctrine of the Immanent Trinity: Dialogue with Karl Barth and Contemporary Theology.* New York: T. & T. Clark, 2002.

———. *Faith, Freedom and the Spirit: The Economic Trinity in Barth, Torrance and Contemporary Theology.* Downers Grove, IL: IVP Academic, 2015.

———. "Love of God and Love of Neighbor in the Theology of Karl Rahner and Karl Barth." *Modern Theology* 30 (October 2004) 567–99.

Muller, Richard A. *Dictionary of Latin and Greek Theological Terms: Drawn Principally from Protestant Scholastic Theology.* Grand Rapids: Baker,1985.

The Night of the Hunter. United Artists. Directed by Charles Laughton, 1955.

Niebuhr, Reinhold. *The Nature and Destiny of Man.* 2 vols. New York: Scribner, 1946.

Nygren, Anders. *Agape and Eros.* Translated by Philip S. Watson. New York: Harper and Row, 1969.

Outka, Gene. *Agape.* New Haven: Yale University Press, 1972.

Packer, J. I. "What Did the Cross Achieve? The Logic of Penal Substitution." *Tyndale Bulletin* 25 (1974) 3–45.

Pannenberg, Wolfhart. *Anthropology in Theological Perspective.* Translated by Matthew J. O'Connell. Philadelphia: Westminster, 1985.

Partee, Charles. *The Theology of John Calvin.* Oxford: Oxford University Press, 1971.

Polanyi, Michael. *Personal Knowledge: Towards a Post-Critical Philosophy.* Chicago: University of Chicago Press, 1958.

Bibliography

Rohr, Richard, OPM. "Incarnation Instead of Atonement." http://cac.org/incarnation-instead-atonement-2017-07-25/?utm_content.
Sanders, John. *The God Who Risks: A Theology of Providence*. Revised Edition. Downers Grove, IL: InterVarsity, 2007.
Schliesser, Christine. *Everyone Who Acts Responsibly Becomes Guilty: Bonhoeffer's Concept of Accepting Guilt*. Louisville, KY: Westminister/John Knox, 2008.
Schmemann, Alexander. *For the Life of the World: Sacraments and Orthodoxy*. Revised Edition. Crestwood, NY: St. Vladimir's Seminiary Press, 1975.
Smail, Thomas A. *The Forgotten Father*. Grand Rapids: Eerdmans, 1980.
Smail, Tom. "Can One Man Die for the People?" In *Atonement Today*, edited by John Goldingay, 73–92. London: SPCK, 1995.
———. *Like Father, Like Son: The Trinity Imaged in Our Humanity*. Grand Rapids: Eerdmans, 2006.
Smedes, Lewis B. *Mere Morality: What God Expects from Ordinary People*. Grand Rapids: Eerdmans, 1983.
Smith, James K. A. *You Are What You Love*. Grand Rapids: Brazos, 2016.
Soosten, Joachim von. "Editor's Afterword to the German Edition." In *Sanctorum Communio*, edited by Clifford J. Green, 304–5. Translated by Reinhard Strauss and Nancy Lukens. Dietrich Bonhoeffer Works 1. Minneapolis: Fortress, 1998.
Speidell, Todd. *Fully Human in Christ: The Incarnation as the End of Christian Ethics*. Eugene, OR: Wipf & Stock, 2017.
Stewart, James S. *A Man In Christ: The Vital Elements of St. Paul's Religion*. London: Hodder and Stoughton, 1935.
Thurneysen, Eduard. *The Sermon On the Mount*. Translated by William Childs Robinson Sr. and James M. Robinson. Richmond, VA: John Knox, 1964.
"To Serve Man." *The Twilight Zone*, March 2, 1962. CBS Television Network. Written by Rod Serling, based on a story by Damon Knight.
Torrance, James B. "New Introduction." In *The Nature of the Atonement*, by John McLeod Campbell, 1–15. Grand Rapids: Eerdmans, 1996.
———. "The Vicarious Humanity of Christ." In *The Incarnation: Ecumenical Studies in the Nicene-Constantinopolitan Creed*, edited by T. F. Torrance, 127–47. Edinburgh: Handsel, 1981.
———. *Worship, Community and the Triune God of Grace*. Downers Grove, IL: InterVarsity, 1996.
Torrance, T. F. *Atonement: The Person and Work of Christ*. Downers Grove, IL: InterVarsity, 2009.
———. "The Atonement and the Oneness of the Church." In *Conflict and Agreement in the Church*, by T. F. Torrance, 1:243. Eugene, OR: Wipf & Stock, 1999.
———."The Atonement, the Singularity of Christ and the Finality of the Cross: The Atonement and the Moral Order." In *Universalism and the Doctrine of Hell*, edited by Nigel de S. Cameron, 225–56. Grand Rapids: Baker, 1993.
———. "The Christian Apprehension of God the Father." In *Speaking the Christian God: The Holy Trinity and the Challenge of Feminism*, edited by Alvin F. Kimel Jr., 120–43. Grand Rapids: Eerdmans, 1992.
———. *The Christian Doctrine of God: One Being: Three Persons*. Edinburgh: T. & T. Clark, 1996.
———. *The Christian Frame of Mind: Reason, Order, and Openness in Theology and Natural Science*. Colorado Springs: Helmers and Howard, 1989.

BIBLIOGRAPHY

———. *Divine and Contingent Order*. Oxford: Oxford University Press, 1981.
———. *The Doctrine of Jesus Christ*. Eugene, OR: Wipf & Stock, 2002.
———. *God and Rationality*. Oxford: Oxford University Press, 1971.
———. *The Ground and Grammar of Theology*. Charlottesville: University Press of Virginia, 1980.
———. *Incarnation: The Person and Life of Christ*. Downers Grove, IL: InterVarsity, 2008.
———. *The Mediation of Christ*. 2nd ed. Colorado Springs: Helmers and Howard, 1992.
———. *Preaching Christ Today: The Gospel and Scientific Thinking*. Grand Rapids: Eerdmans, 1994.
———. *Reality and Evangelical Theology*. The Payton Lectures, 1981. Philadelphia: Westminster, 1984.
———. *Reality and Scientific Theology*. Edinburgh: Scottish Academic Press, 1985.
———." Review of B. B. Warfield." *The Inspiration and Authority of the Bible* in *Scottish Journal of Theology* 7 (1954) 104–8.
———. *Royal Priesthood, A Theology of Ordained Ministry: Second Edition*. 1993.
———. *Space, Time and Resurrection*. Grand Rapids: Eerdmans, 1976.
———. *Theological Science*. New York: Oxford University Press, 1969.
———. *Theology in Reconciliation: Essays Towards Evangelical and Catholic Unity in East and West*. Grand Rapids: Eerdmans, 1975.
———. *Theology in Reconstruction*. Grand Rapids: Eerdmans, 1965.
———. *Transformation and Convergence in the Framework of Knowledge*. Grand Rapids: Eerdmans, 1984.
———. *The Trinitarian Faith: The Evangelical Theology of the Ancient Catholic Church*. Edinburgh: T. & T. Clark, 1988.
———. *Trinitarian Perspectives: Toward Doctrinal Agreement*. Edinburgh: T. & T. Clark, 1994.
———. "The Word of God and the Response of Man." In *God and Rationality*, 133–64. Oxford: Oxford University Press, 1971.
Torrance, Thomas F., et al. *A Passion for Christ: The Vision That Ignites Ministry*. Edinburgh: Handsel, 1999.
Wallace, Ronald. *Calvin's Doctrine of the Christian Life*. Tyler, TX: Geneva Divinity School Press, 1982.
Williams, Reggie L. *Bonhoeffer's Black Jesus: Harlem Renaissance Theology and an Ethic of Resistance*. Waco, TX: Baylor University Press, 2014.
Wolterstorff, Nicholas. *Justice in Love*. Grand Rapids: Eerdmans, 2011.
Wood, Ralph. *The Comedy of Redemption: Christian Faith and Comic Vision in Four American Novelists*. Notre Dame, IN: University of Notre Dame Press, 1988.
Wright, N. T. *The Day the Revolution Began: Reconsidering the Meaning of Jesus' Crucifixion*. New York: HarperOne, 2017.
Ziegler, Geordie W. "The Form of Formation: Trinitarian Participation as the Way of Christian Formation." In *Evangelical Calvinism, Vol. 2*, edited by Myk Habets and Bobby Grow, 339–56. Eugene, OR: Wipf & Stock, 2017.

Name/Subject Index

abide, abiding, 90, 97, 117, 136, 137
    see love _ "abides"
abuse, 19, 20, 72
Academy Awards, 85
"actualist ontology," 60
Adam, 12, 83, 86, 100, 101, 116, 117
agape, agapism, ; *see* love, agape
analogia entis ("analogy of being'),
Anderson, Ray S., 8, 10, 19, 21, 32,
    71, 74, 77, 82, 89, 92, 93, 94,
    104, 105, 119, 121, 124
Anselm, 56, 92
"apophatic reserve," 100
Aristotle, Aristotelian, 48, 106, 114,
    124
Arius, 108
Athanasius, 17, 18, 108
atheism, 90
atonement, 23, 36, 57, 58, 64, 65, 68,
    70, 77, 91, 95–96, 110, 113,
    119, 121
    "Christus Victor" model, 4
    "for us" and "in our place"
        (representative and
        substitute), 23, 58, 78, 91, 98,
        111, 113, 116, 117, 118, 119,
        121, 122
    "in us," 113
    life of Jesus as atoning, 95–96, 102
    ontological, 119, 121 *see*
        ontological
    penal substitutional, 23, 51, 64

    "the perfect penitent" (R.
        Moberly and C. S. Lewis), 113
    see repentance
    recapitulation (Irenaeus), 21, 23
    representative, *see* atonement,
        "for us" and "in our place"
    as satisfaction of the Father, 92,
        93
    substitutionary, 23. 29, 30,
        31, 75, 89–91, 95, 115 *see*
        atonement "for us" and "in
        our place" (representative and
        substitute); atonement "penal
        substitutional"
    theories of, 4, 56
    as *theosis,* 110, 114
    as "wondrous," "wonderful,"
        "sweet," or "sweetest"
        exchange, 114, 117, 123, 144
Atonement (T. F. Torrance), 111
Augustine, 2, 14, 21, 72, 74, 86, 98,
    121
Balthasar, Hans Urs von, 88
Band, the, 120
baptism, 93, 108
    of John, 17
Barth, Karl, 2, 3, 4, 9, 12, 14, 16, 17,
    19, 20, 22, 29, 32, 37, 38, 40,
    41, 50, 52, 53, 58, 60, 62, 67,
    72, 78, 79, 80, 86, 89, 90, 92,
    93, 98, 99, 101, 104, 119
beauty, beautiful, 34, 79, 99
Becker, Ernest, 2

Name/Subject Index

belief, believing, 28, 102, 118, 119 *see* faith
belonging, 28, 36, 119
Berry, Wendell, 18, 117
betrayal, 22, 74, 94
Bonhoeffer, Dietrich, 2, 5, 13, 40, 44, 46, 50, 51, 53, 61, 63, 65, 66, 76, 77, 78, 90, 95, 99, 119
boredom, 32
Calvin, John, 11, 28, 29, 30, 98
Calvinists, 118
Campbell, John McLeod, 9, 53, 73, 109, 110, 111, 114
Cassian, John, 113
Chalcedon, Council of, 44, 119
Christendom, 24. 31
Christian life, the, 28, 88
Christianity, 26, 28, 31, 32, 34, 39, 46, 55, 113
Christology, 23, 61, 119 *see* Jesus Christ
Church, the, 12, 17, 27, 32, 60, 62, 65, 66, 70, 71, 73, 82, 83, 84, 91, 99, 107, 111, 116, 119, 122
    participating in the vicarious humanity of Christ, 81, 105
    as a "vicarious family," 82
Clement of Alexandria, 22
comic books, 80
Communion *see* Eucharist, the
community, 49, 66, 71, 96, 99, 109, 116–20
confession of sin, 111
contingency, 36, 80
Corinthians, First Epistle of Paul to the, 136
covenant, 64, 119
covenant theology, 11
Craig, William, 15
creatio ex nihilo (creation out of nothing), 11, 67
creation, 11, 40, 62, 67, 87, 89, 91–93, 99, 107
    ontological distinction between God and humanity, 78
culture, 77, 91

Cur Deus Homo? (Why Did God Become Human?) (Anselm), 86
Dawkins, Richard, 90
death, 56, 77, 86, 87, 88, 95, 111, 113, 119
Dennett, Daniel, 90
Descartes, René, 72
despair, 19, 29, 47, 48, 74, 76, 91, 97, 102, 119, 144
determinism, 22, 86
Diognetus, the Epistle to, 73
"Distinctiveness and the World," 120
diversity, 91, 99
dogmatics, 2
Dostoevsky, Fyodor, 66
doubt, 19, 105, 123
dualism, 86
Dylan, Bob, 3
Eastern Orthodox Church, 3
Ecclesiastes, the Book of, 47, 91, 92
Edwards, Jonathan, 118
election, doctrine of, 16, 22, 55
eschatology, the eschaton, 57, 58, 61, 109, 111, 116, 119
eternity, eternal, eternal life, 8, 19, 28, 34, 35, 39, 42, 44, 47, 56, 59, 73, 108, 109, 110, 115, 116
ethics, 26, 45, 51 *see* morality
Eucharist, the, 52, 88, 89
Eutychianism, 60
evangelism, 32, 71
Eve, 100, 101
Everly Brothers, the, 91
evil, 58, 81
ex opere operato, ("by the work performed"), 57
"exchange," the "wondrous," "wonderful," "sweet" or "sweetest, *The Epistle to Diognetus*, 114, 117, 123, 144
Ezekiel, 8
faith, the faith, 1, 2, 17, 19, 25, 49, 51, 53, 61, 66, 73, 75, 84, 94, 97
family, 69–84, 143–44
Farrow, Douglas, 60

Name/Subject Index

Fathers, the (early Church), 73, 87, 87, 114, 122
Fiddes, Paul, 37
forgiveness, 21, 53, 56, 57, 59, 60, 63, 64, 65, 66, 77
freedom, 14, 15, 18, 23, 88
  compatabilist vs. libertarian, 36
Freud, Sigmund, 2, 24
Gerstner, John, 118
Gethsemane, 17, 74, 105
God
  as *Abba* "Father," 83
  acts of, 95, 122
  "apprehending" vs. "comprehending" (T. F. Torrance), 107
  aseity of, 121
  attributes of, 56, 88, 137
  being of, 105, 108
  being and acts of, 18, 52, 60, 66, 68, 108, 115, 133
  biblical, 118
  claim of, 67–68
  commands of, 25, 35, 36, 68
  as communion of love, 18, 68, 114 *see* God _ as Trinity
  communion of Father, Son, and Holy Spirit, 63, 108 *see* God _ as Trinity
  and contingence, 36, 80
  as creator, 89
  crucified, 75, 93, 94
  differentiation in, 101, 123 *see* God _ as Trinity
  doctrine of, 114
  economic (immanent) and transcendent (ontological, theological) relationships in the Trinity, 83, 101, 106, 108, 120 *see* God _ as Trinity
  emotions in, 121
  eternal, 74, 93, 97, 106, 107, 108
  essence of, 110
  as Father, 9, 10, 11, 16, 17, 19, 22, 25, 26, 27, 28, 30, 32, 35, 52, 57, 61, 62, 63, 64, 67, 73, 74, 75, 83, 89, 98, 99, 100, 101, 102, 105, 107, 108, 109, 111, 112, 113, 114, 122, 123
  as Father's love for the Son, 16, 22, 54, 58, 65, 76, 96–97, 107
  the Father's "sorrow" over human sin, 123
  the Father's suffering, 111–12
  freedom and love of, 9
  freedom of, 14, 34, 36–37, 88
  grace of, 51
  holiness of, 118
  holy sorrow of, 111–12
  as Holy Spirit; *see* Holy Spirit
  immutability of, 18, 93
  impassibility of, 18, 93
  ineffability of, 50, 108
  kingdom of, 107
  knowledge of, 9, 18, 50, 60, 68, 96, 98, 99, 123–24
  life of, 88, 106
  language about, 180
  as Lord, 19
  as love, 18, 24, 27, 39, 43, 49–68, 76, 81
  as love between the Father and the Son, 6, 37, 43, 44, 45, 52, 58, 98, 118 *see* God _ as Trinity; Jesus Christ _ love of the Son for the Father
  love as essential attribute of God, 118
  love of, 22, 37, 57, 87, 106, 113, 116, 118, 123, 141, 143, *see* love _ divine
  loving, 34, 39, 49–68, 135
  majesty of, 93
  mercy of, 118
  "mystery of God's transcendent being" (T. F. Torrance). 101
  nature of, 8–12, 52
  omnipotence of, 52, 68, 73–74, 96
  omnipresence of, 52
  oneness of, 100, 106
  and "onto-relations" (T. Torrance), 36

133

Name/Subject Index

God (continued)
    participation in the life of, 63 see God _ communion of Father, Son, and Holy Spirit
    "pathos" in, 121
    and *perichoresis* ("mutual indwelling love"), 10, 36, 43, 101, 108, 116
    philosophical pagan ideas of, 93
    presence of, 112
    providence of, 14–15, 92, 107
    revelation of, 9, 101, 102, 105–8
    serenity and tranquility of, 18
    righteousness (justice) of, 110, 118
    as Son, 52, 98, 99, 100, 101, 105, 108, 109, 111, 114, 116, 120–1, 122, 123
        see Jesus Christ _ as Son
    sovereignty of, 10
    as Spirit, 18, 81 see Holy Spirit
    as "the Real" (J. Hick), 57–58
    satisfaction of wounded honor, 56
    transcendence of, 83, 96
    as Trinity (Father, Son, and Holy Spirit triune being), 8, 12, 19, 22, 27, 35, 36, 44, 46, 52, 56, 58, 63, 65, 68, 73, 95, 97, 99, 100, 105–6, 107, 108, 113, 114, 116, 118, 119, 120, 121
        see Jesus Christ _ communion between the Father and the Holy Spirit
    union of the Father and the Son, 17, 44, 52, 61–63, 109
    will of, the, 83
    wisdom of, 118
    Word of, 24 see Jesus Christ _ Word of God
    wrath of, 17, 66, 83, 111, 138
    Yahweh, 86
goodness, the good, 79
goel ("kinsman-redeemer"), 76
Good Samarian, the Parable of the, 58, 59, 62, 63
Gospel of John, the (the Fourth Gospel), 16, 82
gospel, the, 110
Gospels, the, 58
grace, 7, 8, 9, 15, 16–17, 26, 35, 37, 40, 51, 60, 63, 69, 72, 73, 74, 75, 76, 79, 92, 94, 96, 99, 107, 111, 123
    "double movement" of grace, 8, 9, 10, 11, 72, 75, 83–84, 98, 106, 119 see Incarnation _ "double movement" of the incarnation
Gregory Nazianzen, 114
guilt, 73, 94, 121
Harris, Sam, 90
Hart, David Bentley, 121
hate, 19, 21, 113, 83, 110, 119
healing, 94, 119
heaven, paradise, 26, 41, 42, 52, 53, 88, 116, 117
Hebrews, the Epistle to the, 73–74, 82
Heidelberg Catechism, the, 17, 29
hell, 41, 123
Hick, John, 50
Hitchens, Christopher, 90
Holy Spirit, 82, 87, 106, 107, 108, 118, 122 see God _ as Trinity, participation in or communion with, 8–10, 58–82, 108, 116
homosexuality, see love _ same-sex
hope, 47, 61, 119
Horney, Karen, 71
Hosea, the Book of, 25
Hughes, Charles, 50
humanity, human experience, being human, human being, 17, 18, 21, 26, 27, 30, 31, 34, 35, 37, 44, 46, 50, 53, 57, 60, 61, 62, 73, 74, 75, 77, 78, 83, 86, 87, 89. 90, 92, 93, 94, 95, 96, 97, 98, 99, 112, 114, 117, 118, 119, 121, 123,
    autonomy, 39–40, 55, 63, 69, 70, 71, 81, 92,
    as co-humanity, 100
    as creatureliness, 89, 125
    as "crucified humanity" (Ray Anderson), 75, 76

Name/Subject Index

differentiation in, 100–103
and encounter, 89, 100, 102
fallen human nature, 68, 93
"Humans as Sinners/Human Love
  as Tragic," 93–95
the "ideal" self, 71–75
the image of God, 40, 92
  as social, 83
inability, 75
as "I-Thou," 89
the individual, individualism, 27,
  63, 71, 100
and intimacy, 52, 77, 78, 79, 81
judged by Jesus Christ, 70–71
knowledge of, 75, 98
Is love essential to being human?
  85–103
the neighbor, 102
"nomistic existence" (T. F.
  Torrance), 94, 110, 121
and personhood, 83
priests of creation, 87
"redemptive mission in theology
  and science" (T. F. Torrance),
  87
response to God in the Son,
  115–16 see Jesus Christ _ the
  vicarious humanity of Christ
sex and gender see sex
social, 95
as sons and daughters of God, 83
will of, 15, 29, 86, 96
ideology, 90
idols, idol worship, 37, 84
imitation (of God or Christ), 26, 106
Incarnation, the, 4–5, 9, 11, 12, 21,
  25, 27, 36, 44, 46, 50, 54, 60,
  61, 63, 72, 74, 76, 77, 87, 91,
  93, 96, 97, 102, 106, 107, 109,
  110, 113, 115, 119, 121 see
  Jesus Christ
"double movement" of the
  incarnation, "God-
  humanward" and "human-
  Godward," 4, 9, 46, 47, 78,
  79, 97, 106, 108, 119 see grace
  _ double movement of

"double movement" of the Holy
  Spirit, 118–19
inwardness, 52, 79
Irenaeus, 23
Israel, 6, 12, 25, 55, 60, 86
Jayber Crow (Wendell Berry), 41,
  117, 122
Jesus Christ, 3, 5, 10, 8, 12, 13, 14, 15,
  17, 18, 22, 23, 26, 27, 29, 30,
  35, 38, 40, 41, 45–46, 50, 51–
  52, 53, 58, 62, 63, 64, 65, 66,
  67, 70, 72, 73, 74, 75, 76–84,
  86, 87, 88, 89, 93, 96, 97–99,
  100, 102, 106, 107, 108, 109,
  110, 111, 113, 114, 115, 116,
  117, 121, 122, 130
  see Christology; God _ as Son;
  Incarnation, the
  act of God, 46, 60, 121, 122
  as advocate, 98
  apostle, priest, and king, 122
  ascension, 49. 80, 82, 122
  baptism of, 5, 7, 93, 112
  "the Bearer of human mediocrity
    and triviality" (Barth), 98
  as beloved Son by the Father, 5, 6,
    16, 22, 92
  blood of, 56, 64, 75
  buried, 88, 102, d
  and the command of God, 44–47,
    81
  communicatio idiomatum,
    ("communication of
    properties"), 44
  communion between the Father
    and the Holy Spirit, 63 see
    God _ Trinity, the
  confession of our sins, 111
  "contemporary" with
    (Kierkegaard), 87
  "cosmic being," 90
  cross, the, 6, 17, 22, 35, 52, 58, 67,
    70, 73, 74, 76, 77, 84, 93, 97,
    110, 123
    see Jesus Christ _ death of
  crucified messiah, 93, 102
  crucified with, 27, 84

Name/Subject Index

Jesus Christ (continued)
  cry of abandonment on the cross, 6, 22, 67, 70, 87, 88, 89, 93, 110
  death of, 5 6, 102 *see* Jesus Christ _ cross, the
  deity of, 18, 50, 60
  descent into hell, 07
  election of (Barth), 22, 23, 27, 80
  eschatology of, 116–17
  exaltation of, 73–74, 82, 87, 98, 99
  faith and obedience of, 18, 35, 45, 51, 91, 93, 122
  faith of, 14, 31, 45, 61, 73, 75, 84, 107, 111, 114,
  faith, worship, service, and obedience by the Son, 121
  and families, 76–84
  freedom and love, 23
  freedom and obedience, 14, 24, 36
  freedom from "the curse of the law," through his free grace, 94
  friendship, friends, 69–84, 90, 95, 98
  "God becomes human," 87–89
  hearing of the Son, 44–47
  homoousios ("same substance, essence, or being") with the Father, 35, 100, 106, 107–8
  honoring the Father, 63
  humanity of, 5, 22, 24, 60, 65, 75, 97, 111, 112, 116–17, 118
  humiliation and exaltation of, 111–12
  hypostatic union, 119
  identification with humanity, 114
  imitation of, 114
  "inclusive humanity" (R. C. Moberly), 114
  intercession by, 53.65, 108
  "Jesus Christ *is* our human response to God" (T. F. Torrance), 3, 115–16
  joy of, 73
  judgment by, 21

  kenosis ("self-emptying") of the Son, 37, 79
  knowledge of God, 42, 83
  knowledge of love and justice, 54
  laments by, 32, 93, 97
  as Last Adam, 93, 116–17
  as "life-giving Spirit" (1 Cor 15:45), 116
  love command of, 3
  life as atoning, 111, 119
  life of love, 114
  as Lord, 110
  love for the difficult neighbor, 66
  loves in our place, 23
  love of the Son for the Father, 2, 6, 10, 16, 21, 22, 25, 27, 28, 30, 31, 32, 35, 42, 43, 45, 52, 54, 56, 58, 62–63, 64– 65, 66, 76, 77, 81, 84, 85, 89, 92, 95 97, 111, 116
  "man from heaven" (1 Cor 15:48–49), 116
  as mediator, 53, 75, 108
  ministry of, 74, 93, 98
  as New Adam, 21
  obedience of, 18, 51, 52, 56, 58, 63, 74, 83, 91, 107, 110, 114
  offered himself, 88, 114
  "The Original Human," 86–87
  participation in, share in, 78, 110, 114
  perfect Amen of the Son to the Father, 113
  perfect confession of our sins, 111, 114
  "the perfect Eucharistic being" (A. Schmemann), 52, 88–89
  prayers of, 27, 53
  as priest, 27, 82, 109, 126
  "real presence" today (sacraments), 119
  representation by, 23, 53
  response to the Father's love, 107, 115–16
  resurrection of, 29, 52, 78, 117, 119, 122
  revelation of God, 1–7

Name/Subject Index

righteousness of, 68
Sacrament, the, 96
"a servant Lord, a guilty Judge, a wounded Healer" (Barth), 88
"sings the blues . . . for us," 95
solidarity and identification with humanity, 72, 90, 96
as Son, 10, 17, 26, 27, 30, 61, 62, 63, 74, 75, 76, 81, 83, 84, 89, 92, 96, 98 *see* God _ as Son
suffering of, 7, 17, 74, 75
sinlessness of, 74
true man, 86, 99
as truth, 99
union with, 21, 27, 52
union with the Father, 25, 57, 121
uniqueness of, 25, 31
vicarious actions of, 60, 121
vicarious death of, 75, 78, 89
vicarious deity of, 7, 86, 91
vicarious faith and obedience of, 45
vicarious faith of, 25, 27
vicarious humanity of, 2, 3, 4, 9, 11, 13, 14, 18, 20, 30, 31, 32, 37, 39–40, 43, 55, 60, 65, 67, 73, 74, 75, 77, 78, 79, 83, 84, 87, 89, 91, 95, 97, 99, 100, 102, 104, 106, 107, 108, 109, 110, 111, 112, 113, 114, 115, 119–20, 121, 122
see Stellvertretung, Stellvertreter ("vicarious representative action; vicarious act
vicarious life, death, and resurrection, 30
vicarious love of, 25–26, 30, 43, 52, 53, 63, 69–84, 92, 94, 96
the vicarious love of the Son for "flames, friends, and families," 69–84
vicarious repentance (penitence) of, 60, 111–14
vicarious response of, 8, 21, 44, 60, 64, 73, 77, 86, 97–99

vicarious resurrection and ascension of, 122
victory of, 61, 123
will of, 17–18
witness of, 106, 110
as Word of God, 5, 18, 21, 36, 72, 76, 112
worship by, 107, 108, 114
John, Gospel of, the, 95
joy, rejoice, 19, 32, 91, 97, 99, 102, 116, 118, 123
Judas, 74
judgment, 21, 73, 76, 77, 91, 112
justice, 10, 22–24, 54, 63, 64
and love, 19–21, 43, 54, 56, 57, 58, 62
justification, 11, 13, 45, 68, 78, 98, 117
Kant, Immanuel, Kantianism, 34
Kettler, Del and Pat, 1
Kierkegaard, Søren, 11, 14, 16, 18, 19, 22, 23, 24, 25, 26, 27, 28, 30, 31, 33, 34, 38, 39, 41, 43, 45, 46, 48, 49, 51, 53, 55, 62, 64, 67, 85, 86, 87, 104, 109, 116, 120, 121
kingdom of God, 119, 122
Ladd, George Eldon, 40
language, 97, 101
law, the Law, 11, 26, 59, 67, 94, 110, 111, 121 *see* nomistic
Leave It to Beaver, 70
Lewis, Alan E., 52, 88, 93, 94, 102
Lewis C. S., 1, 45–46, 66, 72, 83, 96, 112–13
libertarianism, 74
loneliness, 39, 71, 76, 109
"longings," *(Sehnsucht)* (C. S. Lewis), 32, 47
Lord's Supper, the, *see* Eucharist
love,
 "abides," 87, 90, 117 *see* "abides, abiding"
 as acceptance by others, 40
 as action, 104–5, 122
 agape, 14, 20, 24, 57, 72, 104
 and anger, 18

Name/Subject Index

love (*continued*)
  "believes all things" (1 Cor 3:7), 103
  as belonging to God, 36, 39
  "builds up" (1 Cor 8:1), 104
  Christian, 24, 26–27, 28, 32
  coercive or "no-risk," 8, 9, 22, 36, 58, 104
  as command or call, 23, 29, 35, 39, 44–47, 49, 51, 63, 102
  as communion, 109. 116
  as compassion, 18
  concrete and particular, not abstract, generic, or sentimental, 54, 122
  as demand, 78, 104
  as dependence, 34
  as desire, 2, 14, 32, 64, 69, 79, 99
  as devotion, 35
  as "disembodied love," 104, 105
  as "disinterested love," 24, 111
  and disappointment, 18
  divine, 10, 13, 16, 18, 28, 107, 117
  "does not insist on its own way" (1 Cor 13:4), 116
  as a duty, 23, 34, 35, 55
  embodied, 105
  as an emotion, 21
  of enemies, 10, 26–28
  eros, 8, 13, 14, 20, 24, 25, 28, 31–34, 37, 41–42, 51, 55, 57, 67, 69–84, 86, 92, 117
  essential to God, 88, 118
  "expects nothing" (Barth), 104
  experiences of, 2, 19, 56, 58, 107
  failing, 123
  and families, 19, 69–84
  of the Father, 56, 96–97
  of the Father for the Son, 52, 61
  as a feeling, 68
  and "flames," 69–84
  and freedom, 37, 72
  and friends (*philos*), friendship, 10, 14, 24, 25, 28, 31–34, 37, 41–42, 51, 55, 64, 67, 69–84, 86, 90, 97, 98, 99, 102, 117
  fruits of, 39, 104–24
  as "gift-love," 33, 36, 42
  "hidden life of love" (Kierkegaard), 104
  "Humans as Sinners/Human Love as Tragic," 93–95
  and justice *see* justice _ and love
  and intimacy, 52, 69, 79, 81, 83, 89
  and inwardness, 52
  and lust, 64 *see* love _ as desire
  and marriage, 69–84 see marriage
  as "need-love," 33, 34, 37, 62–63, 105–9
  and mercy, 22
  of the neighbor, 23, 26, 27, 30, 33, 37, 38, 39, 42–44, 47–48, 49–68
  "never ends" (1 Cor 13:8), 117
  and obedience, 6
  objectivity of, 68
  as obsession, 37
  one purpose of, 109–11
  ontological roots, 18 *see* ontological
  and passion, 24, 27, 41
  and paternalism, 64
  possession, 36, 37, 41, 64
  "preferential" (Kierkegaard), 16–37, 41, 42, 55, 61, 62, 64, 68
  promiscuous, 24
  reciprocal, 30, 116
  as reconciliation, 46, 50–51, 91
  as repentance, 53
  romantic, 10, 41, 91, 105 *see* love _ *eros*
  as sacrifice, 35, 41, 53, 58, 88
  same-sex, homosexuality, 55, 70, 76, 81, 82
  and self-denial, 2, 28–30, 31, 38, 44, 66, 79
  and self-esteem, self-image, 28, 30, 38
  as self-love, 18, 25, 27, 28, 34, 38–48, 53, 55
  selfless, 26
  as sentimentality, 51

Name/Subject Index

as "sheer action" (Kierkegaard), 1, 104–5
of the Son for the Father *see* Jesus Christ _ love of the Son for the Father
spontaneous, 34, 55, 72
tragic, 121 *see* tragedy, tragic
and the Trinity, 7–10
as unconditional, 2, 24, 27
and the unmarried, 69–84
unrequited, 8
unselfish, 22
utilitarian *(uti)* and enjoyable *(frui)*, 119–21
as the weeping of tears, 18
"Love as a Response to the One Who is Loved," 115–16
"Love as Sorrow/Sorrow as Repentance," 112–14
"Love in/for the Community," 117–20
Luke, the Gospel of, 83
Luther, Martin, 51
marriage, 3, 51, 70, 71, 72, 77, 81, 82
Marvel comics, 28
Mary, the Virgin, 60
Matthew, the Gospel of, 83
melancholy, 92 *see* despair
Merry Marvel Marching Society, the, 28
middle knowledge, 15
ministry *see* Jesus Christ _ ministry of
Mitchum, Robert, 21
Moberly, R. C. 113, 114
modernism, modernity, 39, 71, 72, 117
Molina, Luis de, 15
Molnar, Paul, 12
Moltmann, Jürgen, 26
Monothelitism, 17
morality, the moral act, 29, 45, 72 *see* ethics
Moses, 38, 66
Myers, Bob, 80
necessity, 36, 94
Nicaea, Council of, 35
Nicene Creed, 100, 101

Niebuhr, Reinhold, 4, 57, 58, 59
nomistic existence (T. F. Torrance), 94, 110, 121
Nygren, Anders, 20, 43, 57, 62, 97
Ogilvie, Lloyd, 29
"One for the Many, the," 25, 31, 53
ontological, 29–30, 81, 82, 87, 108, 119 *see* love _ ontological roots
order, 80, 81, 87
"order of relations" (Barth and Bonhoeffer), 119
pantheism, panentheism 81, 92
paternalism, 19, 20
parents, parenting, 34, 40, 44, 71, 77, 79, 81, 82, 83, 89
Paul (apostle), 11, 14, 21, 27, 66, 110, 111, 116, 117, 123
peace, 110, 118
Pentecost, the Day of, 82, 122
Peanuts (Charles Schulz), 41, 50
penitence *see* repentance
Peter (apostle), 82, 122
Peter, First Epistle of, 116
Plato, Platonism, 26, 101
pluralism, 31
Polanyi, Michael, 49, 119
postmodernism, 31, 55, 69, 70–72
prayer, 53, 66
"presence-amid-absence" (Alan E. Lewis), 94–95, 96, 97, 102
Prodigal Son, the Parable of the, 112–13
Qoheleth, 32 *see Ecclesiastes, the Book of*
reason, 29, 71, 113
reconciliation, 11, 63, 72–73, 77, 91
redemption, 52, 88, 90, 99
Reformed theology, 11, 16
religion, religious acts, 2, 24, 71, 116, 119
repentance, 59–60, 63, 111, 112–14
responsibility, 50, 100
revelation *see* God, revelation of
rights, 20, 21, 62–63, 117
Roman Catholic Church, 3, 66
Rohr, Richard, 121

Name/Subject Index

Ruth, the Book of, 76
sacraments, the, 60, 119
sacrifice, 58, 87, 121
salvation, 16, 57, 87, *see* justification, sanctification
same-sex marriage, 70, 92, *see* love _ same-sex
sanctification, 11, 45, 78, 98
Schliesser, Christine, 56
Schleiermacher, Friedrich, 3, 4
Schmemann, Alexander, 88–89
science, 29, 71, 80, 87
Scottish Theology (T. F. Torrance), 111
Scripture, 28, 97, 107
Semi-Pelagianism, 113
sex and gender, 3, 10, 72, 75, 81, 95, 107
shame, shaming, 73, 112, 121
Sheep and Goats, the Parable of the, 65
sin, sinners, 17, 37, 44, 51, 57, 64, 65, 72, 74, 77, 81, 93–95, 111–14
sloth, 59, 72
Smail, Thomas (Tom), 7, 52
Smith, James K. A., 14
solidarity, 60, 61, 76
Something Old, Something New: Marriage and Family Ministry in a Postmodern Culture (Ray S. Anderson), 71
Soosten, Joachin von, 13
sorrow, 112–14
spirituality, 32, 79, 116
Stellvertretung, Stellvertreter ("vicarious representative action") 12, 50, 51 *see* Jesus Christ _ vicarious humanity of Stewart, James, 52

suffering, 75, 96, 102, 114, 117, 123
    see Jesus Christ _ suffering of
theological anthropology, 86
theology, theological, 17, 56, 59, 80, 87, 88, 99, 117
Thurneysen, Eduard, 45
Torrance, James B., 4, 20, 25, 77, 114
Torrance, Thomas F. (T. F.), 3, 4, 12, 15, 17, 23, 29, 36, 50, 51, 60, 68, 73, 74, 81 82, 87, 94, 96, 97, 98, 105, 106, 106, 110, 111, 120, 121, 122, 123, 124
tragedy, tragic 57, 58, 83, 94, 95, 121
transgender, 81
Trinity *see* God _ as Trinity
Twilight Zone, The, 90
unbelief, 102
undulation, 92, 96
utilitarianism, 64
vicarious act, 50, 60, 66, 75 *see* Jesus Christ _ vicarious humanity of
Williams, Charles, 1
virtue, 45, 58, 86
weakness, 76, 102
Wesley, John, 113
Westminster Confession, 118
Wizard of Oz, The (Baum), 107
Wolterstorff, Nicholas, 19, 20, 34, 54, 56, 58, 59, 62, 63, 64
Word of God, 89, 112 *see* Jesus Christ _ Word of God
worship, 21, 108
Wright, N. T., 40, 51, 78
Yoder, John Howard, 58

www.ingramcontent.com/pod-product-compliance
Lightning Source LLC
Chambersburg PA
CBHW022128160426
43197CB00009B/1187